UNEMPLOYMENT LOOKS BETTER WITH A TAN

Copyright © Adeena Gerding 2023
Illustrations and Cover Copyright © Mary-Anne Hampton 2023

This is a true story based on the real [mis]adventures of the author.
For the protection of the valiant souls involved in this tale,
many names have been changed.
For your sake, many of the diary entries and blog posts included in this book
have had their spelling and grammar corrected.

Every effort has been made to gain the necessary permission of the characters
and materials included in this book.
We apologise for any omissions in this regard and are happy to make the
appropriate acknowledgements and alterations in future publications.

All Rights Reserved.
No part of this book may be used or reproduced by any means graphic,
electronic, telepathic or mechanical. This includes photocopying, recording, taping,
singing, drawing with crayons, or by any information storage retrieval system
without the written permission of the publisher; except in the case of brief
quotations embodied in articles and reviews.
(You are more than welcome to make Adeena famous!)

ISBN 978-0-6397-9522-5 (Paperback)
ISBN 978-0-6397-9523-2 (eBook)

www.bearfootgypsy.com

A catalogue record for this book is available from the *National Library of South Africa*.
228 Johannes Ramokhoase Street, Pretoria, 0001, South Africa

Typeset in Linux Libertine and Open Sans
First Print Edition: June, 2024.

UNEMPLOYMENT LOOKS BETTER WITH A TAN

They told me I could be anything.
So, I decided to be tanned.

Adeena Gerding

For all those whose hearts have led them to strange places.

UNEMPLOYMENT LOOKS BETTER WITH A TAN

Forward

"There's a China woman rowing behind us."

This was our first impression of Adeena, in an anchorage in Namibia, hours before we met this South African/Dutch barefoot adventurer who would join us aboard Sailing Catamaran *Papillon* just two days later, to sail across the Atlantic.

The smiling face on the beach in Namibia was so welcoming, we had to walk over and say hello. Adeena was as friendly as she looked and gave us (the captain and crew of S/C *Papillon*) directions to customs and immigration so we could check into the country. We encountered Adeena several times that day and eventually invited her for a glass (++) of wine on our boat. This barefoot gypsy had many adventures to share with us from her sailing resume. Our captain and his novice crew of three, preparing to continue crossing the Atlantic Ocean from South Africa to the United States, were quite intrigued to learn the experiences this seasoned sailor had accomplished in the previous seven years.

This led us to invite her to join us on our own sailing adventure to which she answered, "Yes!"

UNEMPLOYMENT LOOKS BETTER WITH A TAN

We had Adeena sail with us for over four months to cross the Atlantic in early 2018, and then again for a short sail in Florida in December 2019.

Many other boats were fortunate to have Adeena find them in the years before and after our time together.

Indulge yourself in sailing, bicycling, and hitchhiking adventures around the world with Adeena in the pages ahead. Your life will be enriched, perhaps even transformed, by the unconventional travel stories contained within. (And to start at the very beginning, go read *First We Ate Your Wife*).

Todd and I know how blessed we are to have been in the right place, at the right time to steal Adeena from her original plans and change all our lives for the better. We are thrilled to encourage you to dive into this journey of a life that is definitely better with a tan, whether employed or not.

//Lynn (current first mate) and Todd (current captain) on S/C *Papillon*

Someday in September 2017, I got a request from someone on Warmshowers, a hosting platform for cyclists. A few days later a woman stood in front of me with a big teddy bear and a gas mask attached to her handlebars. She had no shoes and didn't look like the average guest. During her brief stay at my parents' house, Adeena inspired me with her stories and her positive outlook on the world.

About a year later, we embarked on a spontaneous bicycle adventure together. We had left Portugal in October and were on our way to the Netherlands. The further North we pedalled, the colder and the windier it got. Let's say we got to know each other "the hard way."

Somewhere in France I learned that it is better for everyone that she is not allowed to do grocery shopping when "hangry". She once ran around a supermarket like a headless chicken for 20 minutes, only to return with warm beer, chocolate, and a bag of crisps. I found out that Adeena loves cycling as long as it's not uphill, through thick mud, or too cold or wet to be barefoot. Avoiding all this, actually does make it more pleasant.

Despite all the challenges, we made it. Since then, Adeena never left my life and became part of my family. She's the person I call when I need advice about life. It's flipping amazing to have a true friend, a sister like Adeena in my life!

When Adeena enters your life there is a big chance it will become more adventurous. I am sure this book will give you an idea of how awesome life can be with a little more adventure. Adeena has already done the research for you.

//AJ van der Wal

T **he best way to describe my connection with Adeena** would be with a series of emojis: <insert unicorn, glitter, dancers, red wine, cartwheel, laughing face, rainbow, sunshine, surfers, wave, red wine, chips, blissful face, dolphin, coffee, beach, champagne, red wine, disco ball, party, lightning bolt, love hearts face>).

But as that doesn't translate so well to the book medium, I'll give it my best in words…

I remember meeting Adeena for the first time: Sitting with friends at a local Lagos bar, a tanned, barefoot gypsy girl, bounced down the street to join us. Despite having just finished a long work shift, she was radiating energy, glowing cheeks and sparkling eyes.

At that stage, I had no idea that this was the beginning of a beautiful friendship. We gradually got to know each other over countless jugs of cheap wine, beach picnics, "Champagne Fridays" at the farm, dance sessions and other random adventures. She always has an astounding travel story up her sleeve and at some point, we both realised that we are two peas from the same pod.

What I love about her most, is that I can count on her to say enthusiastically "YES!" to every adventure I propose… no matter how sleep-deprived or broke she is.

UNEMPLOYMENT LOOKS BETTER WITH A TAN

She is also very good at orchestrating random adventures. Some include; dancing around a phallic stick at Ponta da Piedade for Midsummer. Going to five parties in a day and doing outfit changes in the backseat of the car between them. Scoping out abandoned warehouses and planning squat parties. Getting up at sunrise for Happy Fit, and crying with laughter about being ok with being totally ridiculous.

I think what unites us is our shared mission. Adeena wants to save people from mediocrity and instead live their lives packed full of fun, crazy, memorable adventures and good times… The contagious energy she holds inspires people on a daily basis, but I now realise that this book is just one of the many ways she is doing this.

//Alexis Bainger, Good Times Lagos

ADEENA GERDING

You have to be careful if you don't know where you are going because you might not get there.

-Yogi Bera

THE JOURNEY

UNEMPLOYMENT LOOKS BETTER WITH A TAN I

PEDALS AND PORTHOLES

1 DO NOT LET YOUR HEART BE TROUBLED 17

2 ADVENTURE BECKONS 27

3 REFUGE IN THE RUBBLE 33

4 DEEP SEA DIARRHOEA 45

5 TRADING BRAS FOR PUMPKINS 51

6 27° SHORT 57

ANYWHERE FOR A HUG

7 REFUGEE 67

8 CONFUSION AND VODKA 75

9 FUCK 83

10 DYSPNOEIC 91

11 HEINEKEN, CHEESE, AND OTHER ABSURDITIES 99

12 TROUBLE BREWS 103

13 THE RULE OF THUMB 109

14 NAVIGATING THE NETHER REGIONS 121

15 LARRY 125

16 STEPPING OUT ONTO THE WATER	129

PIRATE QUEEN

17 ARABELLA	135
18 PAPILLON	145
19 NEPTUNE BE NICE	151
20 FROLICKING THROUGH FRENCH CUISINES	161
21 BAHAMAS BABY	169
22 AND THEN THEY SAID "NO"	175
23 BIG BEAR	181
24 OCEAN BLUES AND BAGUETTES	187
25 FIXING ENGINES WITH POSITIVITY	193
25 WARNING SIGNS OF YOUR GYPSY DEMISE	205
27 HOME	215
000	225
ACKNOWLEDGMENTS	230
ABOUT THE AUTHOR	235

UNEMPLOYMENT LOOKS BETTER WITH A TAN

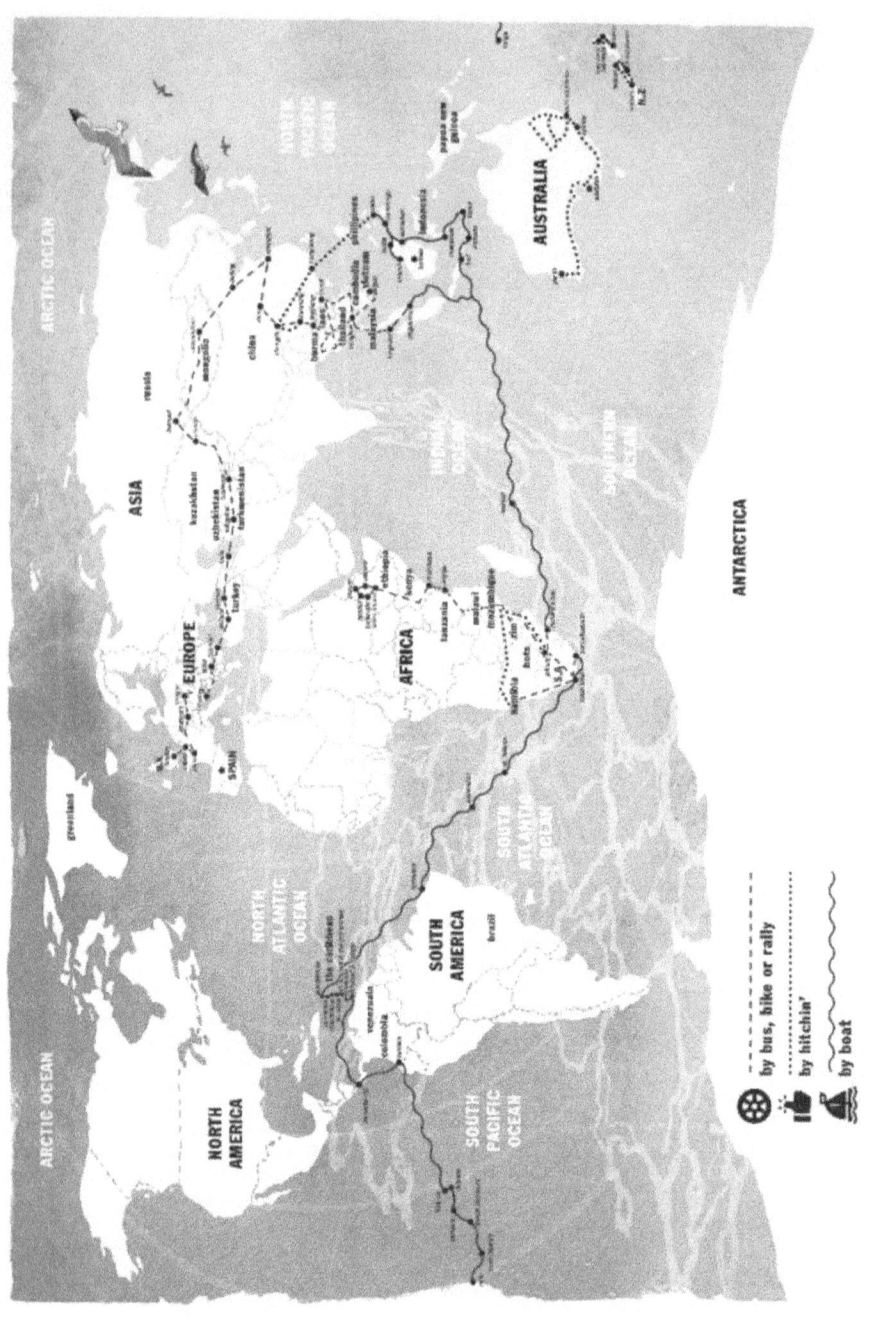

O*nce upon a time,* a long long time ago, I was forced to watch more soccer (call it "football" if you must) than any person ever should. To keep sane, to keep grounded, and to survive my contract at the 2010 Soccer World Cup, I vowed:

> *"I will, starting in Australia, travel over land and sea to whichever country wins."*

And so it was that I hitchhiked from Perth, across the Nullarbor desert, and around the southern contours of Australia. Just when it looked like I was making progress, my hitchhiking ways landed me a job that I actually quite liked. It sucked me in for half a year (apart from a short excursion to New Zealand to gawk at snow and sheep).

I left Australia the day my visa expired and found myself in Southeast Asia with the most inconvenient of parting gifts: Teddy. I faithfully lugged his two kilograms of fluff with me to volcanoes and forests and beaches and parties. We bussed and trained and ferried and hitched and hiked zig-zaggedly across Indochina.

After building (and sinking) our first sailing boat, we experimented with an array of alternative transport before washing up in China, where my mum had since moved to. I found both her and a sudden change of plans.

Instead of turning west, we, the bear and I, ventured through to Borneo to become vegetarian sea gypsies aboard Sailing Vessel *Fiddler*. Despite throwing up most of my vital organs and struggling to keep food down, we ended up sailing all the way home to South Africa. Here, I decided to give the real world another shot.

Settling down lasted only a few months before I found myself being whisked away by the wind again. This time it was Sailing Vessel *Nereid*. Destination: Spain, the country that had won the World Cup.

It was a last-minute decision to cross the Atlantic twice instead of beating [into the wind] up the African coast. The only people who came out to welcome us to the other side of the world were the pirates who pillaged our boat. It definitely was not the best welcome or party we have received. So, Brazil was an interesting experience with mixed emotions.

The Caribbean welcomed us with warm arms. But plans changed again. *Nereid* decided to pause her journey so that the crew and boat could recover. With *Fiddler* only a few miles away, I was purchased from one captain to the other for a pack of cookies (apparently my net worth).

We spent months cruising, diving and exploring the Caribbean as we fixed and beautified the boat. Paradise was ours!

A job offer to film a circumnavigation kicked me out of my comfort zone. I accepted and, to avoid flying, vigilantly scanned Trinidad for any boat heading for Panama. There was only one boat going my way. *Yoldia* was 27-foot long. She had no toilet, fridge or shower; but that only made me want to sail her more. Besides, it was only set to be a two-week trip.

When the circumnavigation was delayed by a year, I gave up on the notion of working and decided to stay aboard the little Swedish vessel with her captain, Karl. While I loved the boat, I was even more attached to her tall, adventure-eyed skipper.

Panama tried to strike us down by throwing bureaucracy, engine problems and hospitalizations at us. Eventually, we managed to get the skipper out of hospital, cross the Panama Canal, and make it into the Pacific.

After countless delays, the longest landless stretch of ocean began. Almost everything that could have gone wrong did. Tired, hungry and coffee-deprived, we grappled with the fact that we might actually die out there.

Fortunately, the will to survive finally resurfaced and a couple of months of deep blue ocean later, we washed up in the most magical place I have ever visited: French Polynesia. Where the trees drip with fruit, the seas swarm with magical creatures, and the people are all smiles.

We found propane, fixed the rigging, and grew leg muscles again while we continued west. In the Tuamotus the crew doubled. It's not so easy squeezing four people into a bathtub-boat. So, in Tonga, Karl resigned his captaincy and we became land people.

We desperately needed jobs and waited out our Australian visas in the capital, Nuku'alofa. When we got bored of waiting and our feet got itchy, we decided to venture closer to "the land of jobs". We arrived in New Zealand with barely a cent to our names.

We hitchhiked for survival and wound up volunteering (read: slaving) until Karl's visa came through. He went ahead.

The continuation of the survival quest landed me and Teddy in prison to enjoy many a sleepless night thanks to the ghosts that shared our cell.

After seven weeks of patience, my visa was finally approved. We fled New Zealand and returned to the "promised land" of Australia. Back to an old job: to the world of kids and outdoor instructing and the shipping container ghetto I called "home".

It took five years and 11 travel diaries to get me straight back to where I had started.

"It has been so long that nobody even remembers the 2010 Soccer World Cup, let alone who won it. But until I think of something better to do, Spain, I am coming for you. "

UNEMPLOYMENT LOOKS BETTER WITH A TAN

ADEENA GERDING

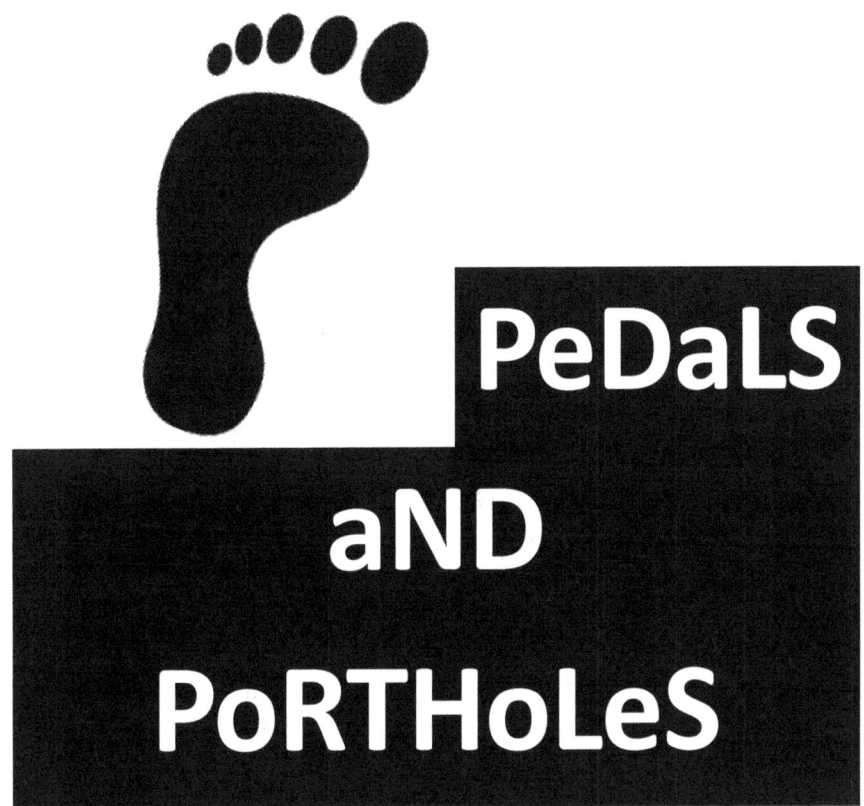

PeDaLS aND PoRTHoLeS

UNEMPLOYMENT LOOKS BETTER WITH A TAN

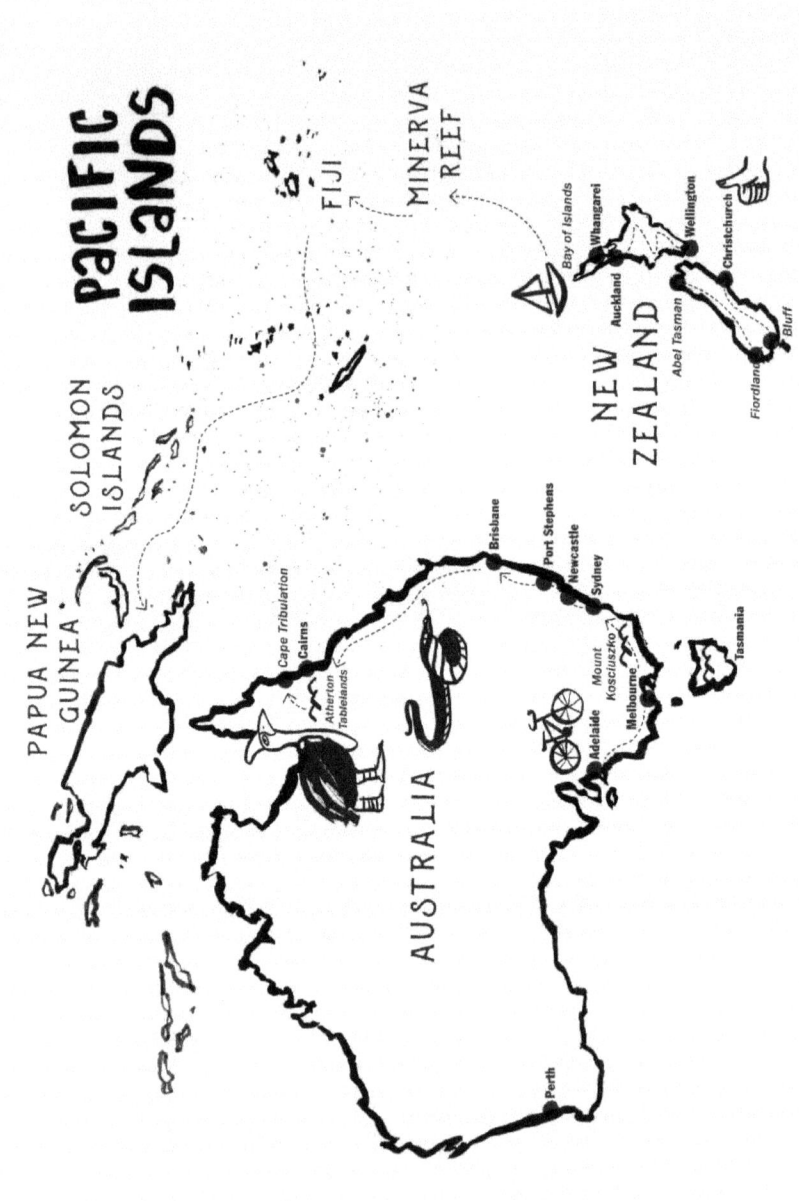

1

Do not let your Heart be Troubled (Pedalling Across the Little Island of Australia)

The *easiest way to deal with heartbreak is to run away from it.* Or better yet, cycle; it's just that little bit faster. With the wind in your hair and the sweat dripping down your brow, you leave your emotions so far behind you that you forget that you even had them.

𝟋

"I'm going to cycle across Australia," I announced, surprising myself as I said it.

Bolts of adrenalin sparked through my being.

"That might be just what you need mate!" said Karl on the other end of the line.

"...and I'm going to do it barefoot," I added.

(Life is always better when you are barefoot.)

"Okay okay, you're officially crazy!" Karl laughed.

We caught up on life and suddenly a new idea came to me:

"... For charity! I might as well do it for charity."

We said our goodnights and verbally hugged each other goodbye from opposite states of the country. I went to bed so excited that I couldn't sleep.

By ten a.m. I had a long list of African charities to consider.
By the afternoon my caring brother had talked me out of it, the African charity thing that is. There just so happened to be an awful amount of corruption and money-pocketing going on in the organisations I'd previously cared for. I turned to Google.

"So, you would like to cycle across Australia for us?" asked Angela, from Bikes 4 Life.

She knew nothing about me and had no idea of the level of crazy she was dealing with. Of course, I wanted to! One look at their mission had me stop Googling:

"It is our mission to collect, restore and provide bicycles to the most marginalised and impoverished communities around the world."

"Do you have a bicycle yet?" asked Angela a couple of weeks later once I was over-committed and dripping in passion for the cause.

"Actually, no, I...."

"Well, you could always ride one of our recycled bicycles," she said with a smile in her voice.

"No training. No support. No shoes." That was my answer to all the naysayers who tried to add reason to my mission.

❦

I'd been in Australia for a few months already and I was getting the subsequent itch that always seemed to surface when I sat "still" for too long. Life was full of great people, fun work, and micro-adventures, but a real adventure had been knocking on my mind's door for a while. And with winter approaching, I knew that I needed to move. It had been years since I had last embraced the season.

I pretended to know what I was doing when I went into the Sydney community Bikes 4 Life workshop to collect my bike. The friendly bunch of cycle-fanatics had all given up their Sunday to recycle bicycles to be sent to Uganda. I became a liability in outsourcing help to transform my newly constructed steed into a continent-crosser.

I cycled out of the warehouse and started my mission, suddenly realising the gravity of the commitment I had just made. I'd done one big cycle trip before, that was an accidental adventure. Psychologically I was prepared for that one; I was in good company. And in every corner of Southeast Asia, you find smiles, shelter and good food! Australia is rather large and has far more wide-open spaces and a lot fewer corners. Not to mention that almost every creature seems intent on killing you.

The cycle lanes seemed to appear and disappear like magic and I ended up mid-traffic over the Sydney Harbour Bridge. People honked and screamed that I wasn't meant to be there. I pushed harder and faster and turned my music up because there was no possible way that I could turn back mid-bridge.

Fortunately, there was a hug waiting for me on the other side. I had a big embrace with Jax and a good night in a real bed. By the morning, I already felt better. Jacqui always seemed to have that effect on me. From our first meeting in Berlin when we had shared a bunk bed in a dorm room. And then, through our lives and heartbreaks in London. And finally in Australia where she was my rock of Zen. And now, the official starting line of my journey.

After a zesty breakfast, I found the correct cycle lane over the Sydney Harbour Bridge and crossed it triumphantly. June 14, 2015, and I was sitting on a recycled bicycle pedalling full-speed across Australia. Well, that's a lie. It turned out to be quite a slow start. Only minutes into the journey, I came to an abrupt halt as a sea of fluff was clouding my rear vision. My teddy bear was already protesting and had forced his leg into the spokes to make it known.

Teddy had joined my life when I had first been in Australia a few years earlier. He had subsequently become my pillow and quite literally a burden to bear. We'd circled the globe together and shared so many [mis]adventures that there was no questioning whether he would be a part of the journey. I even named my charity cycle in his honour: Bearfoot Cycling. The subsequent days all added flat tyres to my trip, slowing me down even more.

I thought it would be easy – you know that whole thing about never forgetting how to ride a bicycle, but it was not. Not when you haven't even touched a bike in three years. Not when your heart is breaking because you have just broken up with your boyfriend over the phone. Not when you actually look at a map and realise that, even though it is just another Pacific Island, Australia is huge!

I stayed at friends' houses for the first three nights. Always arriving much later than I'd promised. Always leaving with a nudging resistance to turn around and give up. By day four, when I'd made it back to the shipping container in Port Stephens that I called home, I was pretty certain that I had to quit. I was not as strong as I used to be. I was not as adventurous as I used to be. I was not as young as I used to be. Fortunately, I was still as stubborn as I used to be. And I never take commitments lightly. After a day of basic supply shopping and butt pampering, I added my eight-dollar tent to the ensemble I had strapped to the rear of my steed and continued.

It rained for the first three weeks. It rained and didn't want to stop. I was drenched all day and even soggier by night. But I was too exhausted to do anything about it. And besides, I was doing it all for a good cause!

I had a few stops with friends, or with friends' relatives, but for the most part, it was just me and the teddy bear and the road. The pain in my buttocks very kindly concealed all my emotional traumas and I simply plundered onwards "for the cause."

The Colliers, some friends I'd had since my childhood in Johannesburg, asked if I would stop near Brisbane to give a talk at their school. The kids had been fundraising for me and they wanted to know all about recycling bicycles and adventure travel.

Helping kids understand how lucky they were and how much impact a simple donation could make, changed something inside of me too. As I pushed my bike and its gear up "the mountain" that stood between me and the school, a new light shone on my journey and somehow filled my path with joy! My muscles still ached and the rain still toppled down on me, but my quest finally transformed into an adventure!

I also realised that just cycling for a charity didn't do much to support them. So, I became proactive and contacted the local newspapers that fell into my path to gain more coverage and raise more funds to get forgotten backyard bikes to the people and communities that desperately needed them.

> *"In remote communities, a bicycle is not only a means of transport to places of employment and education but can provide many with access to remote sources of food, water, medicine and shelter."*
>
> - Bikes 4 Life

The kilometres fell and the detours multiplied. Did I want to cycle an extra 160 kilometres just to see a beach that had a pretty name? Of course! Did it matter that I had to start carrying ten litres of water because I wasn't sure when I'd next be able to refill my bottles? No problem!

I met only one other bike-packer on my route and we shared the road for long enough for him to teach me about other networks that were available to cyclists.

"Have you heard about Warmshowers?" he asked on the first day.

I laughed as I replied, "Of course, I know what a warm shower is."

I didn't have a clue that there was a worldwide network of cycle lovers who were opening their homes and/or their gardens to cycle tourers to allow them the opportunity to have a warm shower.

"If you can keep up," said Austrian Peter, "I'll ask my host if you could join us tomorrow."

If I could keep up!? – That was a laugh! Peter had already cycled across three continents on his trip around the world, how was I supposed to keep up with him?

We turned out to have a similar pace. Apparently, at some point, I had gotten fitter! At the start, an 80 km day took forever. By then I could ride 150 km and still have the energy to explore and to cook dinner at the end of the day!

Riding a bike is a lot like meditation. Your body keeps going through the same motions, keeping it distracted so that your brain can focus on other things. Like the koalas that clung to the trees, there are little treasures to find in your mind's eye. And like the trees that span the endless roads of Australia's East Coast, your brain continues to open up old chapters that you never properly dealt with. At other times it's simple happy memories that fill your horizon.

"Cyclists see considerably more of this beautiful world than any other class of citizens. A good bicycle, well applied, will cure most ills this flesh is heir to"

– Dr K.K. Doty

There was nothing in the way of cycle lanes. In the first quarter of the journey, I could detour through forests or fire trails to escape the road. Later it was just hundreds of kilometres of stretches shared with road trains and occasional cars. Once I'd entered The Tropics, the snakes became plentiful. This is where having poor eye-sight became rather challenging, I could never tell if it was shreds of tyres or sunbathing snakes lining the road shoulder. More than once a cobra spiked up to hiss at my bare feet.

There were times when I felt like there was no possible way I could finish, and I was certain that I needed to throw in the towel. But then, from nowhere, motivation would arrive. Sometimes simply sitting down on the side of the road and having a sandwich would have me restored. Other times the yells of encouragement from passers-by speeding past in their cars, trucks and campers would give me umph to make it up the toughest hills.

Flat tyres and breakdowns were regular occurrences. But instead of looking at every blowout as a punch in the face, I saw them either as life lessons or opportunities to meet caring strangers. The world is full of caring strangers.

I pedalled on and on and my heart started beating again, and not just from over-exertion! By the time I was 80 km away from Cairns, my final destination, I wasn't ready to finish. There was only one way to dodge it and that involved a mountain range. I rode straight up and over the Atherton Tablelands, something my legs would have deemed impossible at the start of my trip. I kept going and going – North, always North. Until eventually there were only dirt roads and the 4x4s that flew down the track seemed determined to either kill me or camouflage me with dust so that someone else could. I suddenly had peace and felt like I was ready to finish my journey. And I was excited for what lay ahead.

I turned around and cycled South. Straight into a cassowary, the world's most dangerous bird. They're known to attack with both their beaks and the claws on the backs of their legs. I'd overcome my fear of tomatoes a few years prior and since then, for some reason, my nightmares always involved being pecked to death by birds. The bird and its young walked circles around me and my statued bicycle as I held the brakes trying not to roll downhill. My heart, which was finally beating again, rang out like a jackhammer in a library. Once around, twice, the mum was giving me the once-over. It stepped closer and a car pulled up. The birds ran away. I continued my journey trying to take stock of my life.

I know I have guardian angels protecting me. There's no way I would otherwise have survived so many wild, near-death encounters. I thought back to a miraculous escape from hijackers where I drove straight through a vehicle. I thought back to running into a leopard, it's not by chance that the leopard blinked first. I thought back to camping on the Botswana border with my brother and how somehow the lions circled but did not harm us. And more recently, the pirate attack where I was the only one left completely untouched. There were definitely angels watching over us as we sat adrift in the Pacific. I pedalled on realizing how lucky I was to be alive. And I realized how good it was to fully live.

Jax met me at the finish line with balloons and hugs and a week in Cairns celebrating life. And the finish line was like the starting line, except I was a completely different human. One who believed that everything was possible. One who didn't mind conquering mountains. One who was ready to take on the world!

I donated my bicycle and hitchhiked the shorter, inland route back to work. Inland Australians seemed to be a lot more dubious and weirder than the ones I had met along the coast. There were a few sketchy rides, but I was strong, my mind was clear, and I was a survivor!

I may have been ready to take on the world, but I was not ready to be back in my little shipping container. Heartache still loomed there like a disease, suffocating me by day and plaguing me with nightmares by night.

Living with 40-something other people had its excitement and its perks. I'd talked so many other people through their troubles.

"So, you're pregnant…"

"Syphilis…"

"He cheated on you…?"

"Syphilis…"

"You're homesick…"

"You're fired…."

"…syphilis???"

But when it came to mine, I didn't feel like there was anybody I could open up to. So, I didn't. And when the opportunity arose, I fled!

2

Adventure Beckons

"*What do you mean you don't have any plans?*" asked one of my younger colleagues that I didn't know particularly well.

"Well, I was just going to see what happens when I get there. Maybe walk across Tasmania or something."

Before I knew it, Georgia and I were hiking across Tasmania together. And I didn't know it at the time, but Georgia was probably the best thing that could have happened to me. We shared broken hearts and common faith. She had at least fourteen times the energy I had, but we made excellent adventure buddies for each other.

Until Queenstown that is. We'd finished our walk and were doing a circumnavigatiory hitchhike of the island when we got stuck. The town petrified us. And the inhabitants even more so. We dreaded having to spend another night there, but there was no through traffic and our thumbs didn't seem to be working. There was a weekly bus, but that had left the previous day. It was getting late when a friendly Canadian pulled up. If there is anything I have learned from spending long hours awaiting a hitchhike, it's that there is somebody you need to meet on the other side. We needed to meet Dave.

He was dripping with passion for life and love for his family. He had met his wife after hitchhiking around Australia. He had been through a lot but had decided what he really wanted and had chased that. He listened to our stories and told us his. Something changed in both of us and the things that happened in our last days in Tasmania were nothing short of magical!

His words stuck with me all through Tasmania. And as we hitched to the airport. And as our flights were cancelled. We discussed them over dinner in our free, multiple-star hotel. And we held onto them as we returned to Sydney. I hugged Georgia goodbye at the airport. She had some things that she needed to sort out. So did I.

My visa expired, so I fled, but Australia was not done with me yet. After some mandatory Southeast Asia adventures, I returned to ride a bike for the very same charity, only this time there were 60 of us doing it together. It's amazing how much more fun there is to be had in having a team working towards a common cause. I may have been the only one without cleats (I was barefoot, of course) and it may have been the very first time I sported Lycra, but I tried not to let that bother me.

Stiff and sore from the ride down The Great Ocean Road, I returned to Melbourne to meet my baby brother, Jeandré. He was craving adventure, so we hiked the southernmost regions of Australia. We didn't have much time so we did a marathon walk and a few sketchy hitchhikes[1]

---

[1] When hitchhiking, do not get into the car when your driver has a penis drawn on his forehead. He may just be part of a bachelor party and he may have simply been looking for a toilet, seen your thumb, and decided to help.

before driving a relocation campervan[2] to Sydney. We stopped to climb Mount Kosciuszko, gawk at pretty things, try and cook roadkill, and lick random artefacts. Sydney was the meeting point for our first family reunion in three years. Brendon, the babiest of my brothers, had just moved there and we had flown Mum in from China for her birthday. Australia probably was not prepared to have so many Gerdings gathered together in one place!

My flight was delayed twice, so at least I could hug mom goodbye at the airport. I walked her to her gate then she followed me back to mine, then hers... we danced around the airport with tears in our eyes. She was headed back to China and I was on to new adventures.

༺

Vince met me at the gate with a beard full of smiles and a bag full of beers, crisps and camping gear that he had managed to ascertain from various strangers and bins around the airport while he had patiently waited for me. But he also carried some bad news: we weren't allowed to sleep at the airport. With all the delays, I'd told my friend Steph that we'd meet her in the morning rather than her having to do a ridiculous o'clock airport run.

We ventured outside to find somewhere to pitch our tents and ended up napping on the traffic circle just exiting the airport. The ring of trees it sprouted made for perfect shelter and a great spot to catch up and savour beers. Unfortunately for Steph, it also offered no cellphone reception, so when she did come to collect us, she couldn't find us.

Steph was like a sister to me. She'd taught and debauched me the first time I had been in Australia. I didn't know Vince well, but I liked him. He was just about the right level of crazy to adventure with. He was one of the many housemates I'd recently lived with while in Australia. I once organised a beach campout and a sunrise hike. Despite everyone's enthusiasm, he was the only one that actually showed up. It later evolved that he had a similar addiction to adventure, hitchhiking, and the outdoors.

---

[2] Did you know that you can get a free campervan simply by going against the grain? Everyone was driving from Sydney to Melbourne and nobody was driving back, so we were fortunate enough to deliver one back to Sydney. When you are really lucky, they will even pay for your fuel.

We both needed post-Australia plans, so we met up in Christchurch and started New Zealand together.

It was so cold that we walked into the local charity store to restock our wardrobes. Hitchhiking in onesies became the new normal. And the beautiful array of people who crossed our paths (both old friends and absolute strangers) completely agreed that life was better in a onesie!

We had some of the most bizarre and awesome adventures all through the South Island. Vince eventually accepted a seasonal job in his hometown in Canada so we decided to end our adventure with a kayak trip. A sporadic storm hit and while all the hikers were evacuated from the Abel Tasman National Park, we were left battling the elements. Hiding in a sheltered cove, I warned him that by returning to Canada, he would find love and a puppy and possibly never leave again. I'm not even a fortune-telling gypsy; but words do have power.

My adventures continued through a tapestry of beautiful people as I headed North. I planned to find the perfect spot to restock my bank account and utilise my Working Holiday Visa. Plans seldom follow through (at least when it comes to me and adventures).

New Zealand has more boats per capita than any other country in the world. And despite my best intentions, I could not deny the allure of the ocean. It called my name, and loudly. And, as we all know, when adventure beckons, we must heed its call! Besides, unemployment always looks better with a tan. And what better place to work on your tan, than on a boat?

I wasn't sure that I'd find a boat out of New Zealand. And I wasn't sure where exactly I wanted to head for afterwards, so I checked into a hostel for the night and took a walk down to the Whangarei Marina to have a look at the noticeboard. Before I knew it, I was on a boat celebrating a birthday. I met a dozen colourful people and I met Renate. The following day, I moved onto her boat. I didn't realise how much I had to learn from her, but over the next few weeks, we developed a sisterhood.

Renate had lost her husband a couple of years earlier and hadn't moved the boat since. There was a lot of work to be done in getting Sailing Vessel *Renahara* sea-worthy. She wasn't heading anywhere quite yet, but

Renate wanted to be ready for adventure when it summoned her. She dreamed of sharing her sailing passion by taking a boat full of women for a circumnavigation of the Pacific the following year. I was happy to share her home and workload with her while I decided what I wanted.

Despite my early concerns, I had long queues of people lining up to offer me a spot on their vessels. New Zealand had just changed their rules and any boat wanting to depart for international waters needed crew with at least 3000 miles of blue water sailing experience. Most of the local competent sailors didn't have that. Other people just wanted company or were sailing with kids and wanted an extra set of trustworthy hands around.

"We need a captain!"

The statement took me a bit off guard, but I was listening.

"We have a boat, but none of us has really ever sailed."

The owner was dripping with goodness and she had me intrigued. I ventured over to meet the rest of the crew: six exceptionally intelligent and creative hippies from six different countries. I spent days working with them and getting to know them while making the decision. But every day I had other sailors pulling me aside and trying to talk me out of it:

"What if you have a collision or someone dies? Are you ready for that kind of responsibility?"

"What if they bring drugs? – You are the captain; you know you will be responsible."

"Do you trust the boat? Do you know anything about its history?"

Paid positions started emerging but I knew where my heart was and I wasn't going to let other people's fears get in the way of the path I needed to follow. It was time to up my game and step out of my comfort zone. I headed over to the boatyard to give the crew the affirmative.

At the bottom of the ladder, my phone rang.

"Is that Adeena?"

A 100-foot gaff rig schooner wanted me to hop on board as the sailing instructor as they carried backpackers to Fiji and then on to Vietnam. "Vietnam!" "Backpackers!" "Gaff rig!" I didn't even think about it, I said "Yes!"

UNEMPLOYMENT LOOKS BETTER WITH A TAN

3

Refuge in the Rubble

We *don't have enough beds, so you will have to share with me,"* said Tony, the captain.

I should have seen the warning lights straight away, but instead, I built myself a bed on the shelf in the living room. A Gypsy makes a plan. Adventures were beckoning and I was all in!

I had a few days to go before we were to set off, so I enjoyed some more of Renate's brilliance. When it finally came to departure time, a fellow boat hitchhiker arrived to inquire about doing a passage on *Renahara*. There had been many of them walking the docks, but Ben was different. We both agreed that he would have better luck finding a boat in the Bay of Islands rather than Whangarei. Seeing as Renata was giving me a ride to my new job, we told him to jump in the car too. Ben, the mousy-brown curly-haired dancing-heart from Austria, and I had crossed paths several times already. It was nice getting to know him better on the car ride. I gave them both the tour of my new home, *Schooner Havsström* before I hugged Renata goodbye and Ben ventured off to boat hunt. He returned later with a kiss.

The crew started boarding. Finnish Hans, the smiling co-owner and carpenter of the beautifully manicured wooden vessel. Then Bette, the joyful, soulful Dutch woman taking a break from her busy work life to oversee provisioning and our galley. Damien, a French adventurer, had spent weeks working on the boat to get it ready and was overjoyed to finally be departing. And the backpackers. 12 of us in all.

I gave everyone a basic introduction to sailing. I explained how we would use the wind to navigate our course towards Fiji. I gave the rules: "One hand is always to be holding onto the boat. You always have to be clipped on if you are in the cockpit at night. Don't put anything down, it will fall over. Don't change course without first consulting me or the captain. Keep a watch out for other boats, storms, mermen and any hazards that we would prefer not to collide with." I warned them that if they fell overboard, they would probably be goners. And most importantly, I taught them always to puke and pee to lee (never into the wind). And then I started learning very quickly how the gaff rig worked so that I would always be one step ahead of the backpackers. It's hard work raising and changing those square sails, but it was fun.

Captain Tony didn't like fun. There was an unwritten rule that it was not allowed on board. As soon as somebody was enjoying themselves or any glimmer of laughter filled the air, Tony would rush over to extinguish it. Hans was his complete opposite, but even between them, we could all feel the tension.

I needn't have explained the hazards of sailing as we didn't do a lot of it. The water was glass and the motor was the only thing driving us forward. Swimming laps around the boat was a daily activity. Tony downloaded daily weather charts, but instead of getting in the path of the wind, he chose to steer us to where it had been. The two of us were hardly in the same book, never mind on the same page. Unfortunately, we did share the same boat.

The engine strained under the weight of the hefty vessel as we pushed forward. Exhausting both the primary fuel pump and its backup, we found ourselves replacing it with a water pump that demanded constant cooling from our precious freshwater reserves to prevent it from succumbing to the heat. The engine was the only one getting a shower on route, or any fluid at all. Tony tyrannized over our water supply. He claimed, "The backpackers are using too much," while cooling the engine wasted gallons of water every day.

Tension was high onboard seeing as laughter was outlawed, but there were still beautiful moments, meals and magic shared amongst the rest of us. I thought it might be fun to have a break in Minerva Reef on the way; to lift spirits and allow everyone a full night's sleep. But Tony had never heard of Minerva and therefore it did not exist. I dug out all my digital charts, sailing guides, maps, and pictures from my previous Pacific sailing and put together a nice presentation. Tony still took convincing.

We caught a fish on the way in, but a shark bit the body off while we were reeling it in. And the second catch was the same. But those were reef sharks, right? What harm could reef sharks possibly do to humans? Fortunately, we only heard the horror stories much later and were carefree as we busied ourselves with kayaking, diving, and a feast of fish remains. Wine was allowed, and so was laughter. It was a good night. We even managed to trade a bottle of rum with another boat in exchange for a fuel pump.

Although there was a second day of activities planned too, the wind arrived with a storm. A few of the other boats had taken refuge in Minerva to escape the storm, but Tony was wind-hungry and wanted us to ride it out. Leaving the reef had me riding the mechanical bull of the bowsprit while freeing up the headsail. We plunged through the waves while almost colliding with a whale. The others were awed and jealous. I was happy to be alive.

We arrived in Fiji at last. After only 14 days, it's amazing how much I missed land. I licked it in gratitude and we all ventured into the land of a million smiles. On the land, there was no hierarchy and we all had an epic night celebrating our arrival in Savusavu as equals.

*

"I'm leaving," said Damien, "and you should come with me."

He had a point. I wasn't liking the way the boat was run and I valued the joy of my soul and... But then again, it was a job and I had so much stuff. Not only my gypsy belongings, but boxes of wine and chocolate, and other essential goods that the Pacific islands were known to be lacking.

"Ummmm…"

He was just about ready to leave and I was still "umming". I hugged him goodbye and told him I'd catch up. But when? How did I ask Tony to leave? I didn't want to let anybody down.

If there is one thing I have learned since, it is to follow your soul/guts/heart/instincts. Whenever something inside you speaks loud enough, you need to listen to that thing. If you don't feel good, get out! I wish I knew that then! I wish I had realised that I was a mere mortal, easily replaced. I wish I cared more about what I thought about myself than about other people's ideas and impressions. I stopped overthinking for a moment because a new boat was arriving in the anchorage and Ben sailed in. That simple kiss had left a lasting impression that had drifted with me across the Pacific and my heart was a disco drum as he waved his way past.

Two days later we both quit our respective boats. I sat on the bow that night and star-gazed. I almost cried. My life was on the crest and the trough at the same time. *Tomorrow will be the start of a brand-new chapter for me and I don't have a title for it or any idea what it will hold.* I shoved my things into my bags and piled them in the corner before crawling onto my shelf-bed. I tried to slow my brain and heart and soul to a rest state. But morning came far too quickly and I was not ready for it. At least I had Ben. And since we didn't quite know where Damien was, we started hitchhiking to find him.

Thursday 2 June, 2016.

How I ended up here, I am not entirely sure. I am sitting on a postcard beach sipping a coconut in a mangrove with my sudden husband, watching the villagers pull in their afternoon catch of ika (fish). Three days of yacht-free living evidently goes a long way!

My new parents, Litiana and Josefa, keep fattening me up with delicious treats and fried foods. And even though I have only known them for a few days, we are family.

Instead of existing in a fake world of luxury, Vatulele has thrown smiles and happiness and a banquet of real life in my direction.

We came here to see a village and got sucked right into a community.

Hitchhiking turned out to be much more difficult than expected. The only vehicles on the road were buses and taxis. We eventually gave up and boarded a bus. Only seconds later, a woman approached, introduced herself and started chatting. Before we knew it, we were disembarking with her and a few others, headed for their village. I fumbled along chatting to some woman while Ben followed with the others.

"Is that your husband?" they had asked excitedly.

"No, I just met him a few days ago," I replied earnestly, laughing.

We were made presentable in skirts and shoulder covers and taken to the local chief. For foreigners (or any outsider for that matter) to enter a village, they have to become part of it. We rummaged through our bags for some of the gifts we had thought to carry and followed. Sat in a circle we followed their chant and drank the kava they had mixed for the occasion.

"Welcome brother Ben and sister Tina."

Nobody could ever get my name right, so "Dina/ Tina" was just fine. We clapped a lot and became part of the village.

After sitting through several gift-giving (sevusevu) and grog drinking (kava: dry mildly-sedative roots mashed up with a pestle and mortar, and soaked into water) ceremonies where my name and a lot of clapping gets thrown about almost haphazardly, I came to realise a few things. Firstly, I didn't like kava very much. Secondly, I found a more accurate depiction of who I was. In Fijian "Dina/Tina" means "true and genuine." And I'll take that! Even if I was living a bit of a lie. Ben had answered the marriage question quite differently that first day, so I was always introduced as his wife.

Fiji had recently been ravaged by Cyclone Winston. Houses were destroyed, and crops were lost, along with lives. Everybody had a story to tell about how they endured Winston's pillaging.

"We were sitting in our home, and the wind started to pick up. It gets stronger. Stronger. Stronger still. Before we knew what was happening, the whole house began to tremble, and our roof got whisked away. We clustered together as a family and ran to the neighbours, but their house wasn't there anymore so we kept running. The community hall... We find solace for a second, but the concrete starts disintegrating, so we club together again and run for our lives. The only protection we could find is an uprooted tree. With eight of us hiding in its roots, we knew our chances were slim..."

"We heard there was a storm coming, so we'd battened down the shutters. Three families sat inside sipping sugary tea and eating custard tart [a national pastime]. The rains were bucketing down outside, but our house was strong. We think we're safe. In an instant, water comes gushing through the living room and we're in it. Struggling for breath, we follow the flood, fight the currents, even though we can't swim..."

"The walls are shaking and we have no idea what to do and we have nowhere else to go. We sit and sing and pray. We've got all the generations of the family in our house and we know that at any second we could all be face-to-face with Saint Peter or whoever it is that controls Heaven's admission list. The wind pounds on the door and roof for hours, threatening to enter. When nobody answers, it leaves, only to return with more force. When it's finally safe to peek outside, we find we're the only house left standing."

We had a lot of work to do rebuilding and planting crops. We enjoyed lending a hand while learning the cultural norms of Fiji. Fiji was so much more than just the honeymoon destination that I had envisioned.

The women seemed to be the most productive in our first village, they worked hard. From harvesting at dawn to fishing at night. While the men sat in circles sipping kava and exchanging stories. I loved working with the woman, but I also enjoyed hearing the stories as the kava cup was dipped and passed around. Village life was interspersed with daily church services and sugar.

Not wanting us to go astray, our exceptional hosts called up their family near Labasa and told them we were coming. We arrived with even more vegetables and a bigger bunch of kava. The village was tucked away between an oil refinery and a sugar plant. The kids played with whatever they found washed up on the shores (crabs, syringes, diapers, etc). When we arrived, we were immediately treated like royalty (only instead of a red carpet, we had straw mats). We were living amongst the poorest of the poor and they were lavishing us with luxuries. It was impossible to do anything without having seven or 19 children hanging off your arm. They all wanted to be our friend. They all wanted to bring us fresh coconuts from the highest palm trees. They all wanted to make sure that our daily hug quota was filled. If I went to the bathroom, they would wait patiently outside; and when I braved the shower, they'd poke their eyes through every gap in the corrugated iron walls. In the morning I'd see their shadows lurking around my tent waiting for any sign of life. They had the most beautiful voices and, with a diet of mostly sugar, more energy than the power station down the road. Again, the village gave us everything and took nothing in return. Again, I felt like I had to flee - my heart would burst if I had to accept any more generosity!

We continued around the island, being adopted by new villages and getting used to the mandatory kava offerings as we went. Somebody always had relatives somewhere to send us to. It didn't matter how poor the family was, they always had more than enough to share! We always tried to share our bounty, but they would simply prepare it and serve it to us, making us feel pangs of guilt for imposing ourselves on them. In Fiji, it is cultural to share what you have. As a village, everything is communal. A way of life that most of the Western world has forgotten.

We worked hard where we could, and tried to motivate action where we could not. In some villages, there was a mindset of living simply for the day and never thinking about tomorrow. Their houses were semi-reconstructed, or they were living in tents donated by the UN. For today that was enough. Similar to the crops. All the affected villages had been donated six months' worth of food to give them time to sow for the future. But some villages didn't seem to be in any hurry to do farm work when food was so readily available.

One thing every village did share was their love for sugar. And even if the tea was prepared with an insane amount of sugar already added, they would still lump several tablespoons of the powder into their cup. The tart was delicious. Sometimes it was breakfast. Sometimes it was lunch or dinner or both. Sugar became our staple diet.

Any initial romantic pangs that had lingered between Ben and I were quelled by facing the harsh reality of post-cyclone life. There was so much happiness in the souls of the Fijians, but sadness lingered in the rubble.

Damien finally found us at the far end of the island where we planned to take a ferry over to Taveuni. The Frenchman was alive with joy and excitement from having learned and experienced so much. His presence made us realise just how broken we had become. And it offered a reset before we carried our frustrations through to new territory.

We arrived on the new island with little in the way of plans and simply drifted from place to place learning, building, and enjoying. The Fijians know how to live!

Ben accepted a formal volunteering position and ventured off to lend a helping hand while Damien and I continued to uncover the wonders of Fijian life while trying to assist.

"Should we grab some groceries first?" I asked as we clambered on yet another bus.

"Nah, everything we bring gets given back to us and I'm tired of having things go off in my pack. There'll be a shop anyway..."

We weren't sure where we should be going, so we asked the bus. There was a unified agreement amongst the other passengers that we should be going to Navakawau. So, we did.

We arrived in the dark, and Rosi, who I'd sat next to on the bus, told me to follow her. We walked through a tented camp and into her brother's home which was reconstructed from debris to a third of its original size. It now housed two families with nine children.

"Winston stole our house," she laughed.

They shared their evening meal with us and poured us tea. Apart from being the worst-hit village on the island (25 of 135 houses were salvageable), the chief had just died. It appeared that our timing couldn't have been any worse.

Sat in their China-Aid tent (they wouldn't let us pitch our tents in the dark), we cried. Here we were in the worst of the worst disaster zones, and we'd arrived empty-handed. We cried for what they had lost in the cyclone. We cried because even though they had nothing, they were giving us so much. We cried because their chief had just died on the same day and it was a day of mourning. We cried because we didn't know what else to do. We were simply adventurers curious about the world. These people were fighting for survival.

What a difference a day makes! As we had our morning intake of sugars, we watched hordes of people lining up to meet the former chief's brothers with offerings. We had simply brought a few dry smelly kava roots, but people from distant villages were arriving with bundles of cassava, kava, vegetables, whalebone, and pigs. We had planned to flee at the first opportunity, but the opportunity never presented itself as we were put straight to work preparing funeral food.

The far south of the island, where we were now tribesmen, was the worst we had seen. Not a single coconut remained on the trees. The rubbled remains of former homes were everywhere. But we somehow managed to stop looking at what the Fijians didn't have and instead saw what they did have. Winston stole their roofs. Winston stole their houses. Winston stole their power, their water, their family heirlooms... but Winston left them with their lives, and they knew how lucky they were. Watching how they worked together to construct shelters and do food preparations for the ten-day funeral made me realize that Winston had actually brought them closer together.

There was always something to do, whether it be construction, vegetable chopping, or making thousands of pancakes (which I did for three days straight). I blended in so well that most of the funeral guests spoke Fijian to me. Everyone had stories, similar to the ones above, to tell of how they had survived the cyclone. You could see why they believed in God. Everyone also had something to teach, and at the same time, everyone wanted to learn what they could from us.

I can't tell you about normal proceedings, but for a chief, a Fijian funeral is very elaborate and spans eight to ten days. And every meal at this time is a shared meal. We quickly upped our Fijian skills as we prepared food, washed dishes and mingled. We drank kava with friends we knew from every corner of the island and all the new friends that we were constantly making. We moved into our own tents to allow space for all the new visitors. They had never seen such tiny tents in all their lives! The kids found them hilarious and we always had hordes of visitors and peeking eyes.

I'd recently written a blog about how I got lost in the world. In reality, I had found myself in Fiji. The people were the friendliest I'd ever met and the smiles were by far the biggest. The generosity of the villages has been unparalleled. But it was also one of the most difficult countries I'd travelled in. Every stop made me look deep within and showed me things I didn't want to see. It challenged me about my own motives. It made me learn how to accept things. It's a country that wrestled with my heart and my soul and brought me out with a new outlook on what truly is important in life.

We left, not feeling like we had pillaged the village, but with renewed souls and a motivation to give and lavish love. Our lives seemed to carry a new purpose. I carried this with me to further islands and back to Savusavu where I bumped into a friend from New Zealand. He was sailing out to rebuild communities with a charity. Did I want to join?

𝒇

Damien headed off to New Caledonia and I headed back to the world of boats. I plastered a sign saying that I was looking to crew onwards, and once again I was met with a host of options. I did join up with my friend Dave to volunteer with an organisation while I tried to make good life decisions.

But...

But working with an organisation could not have felt more wrong for me. The heart behind it was amazing, and the sailors involved were doing exceptional work rebuilding a school. But it was us and them. It was as if they thought that we had been brought in to fix their problems. And instead of working alongside the islanders, as I was now accustomed to, our only interaction was when they served us tea. Or when we needed to take boats to other islands to get supplies.

But...

But there were so many questions racing through my head about the future that it was hard to be in the present.

But…

But was Ben right? When he had left, we had had a very honest conversation about the things that bugged us about each other. Things that we had not been previously aware of in our own behaviours. How could I change? What could I do to become a better me? I wanted to make a difference on this planet, but the first thing I needed to change was myself.

UNEMPLOYMENT LOOKS BETTER WITH A TAN

4

Deep Sea Diarrhoea

Yacare, *the crocodile.* I think I was mostly attracted to her because she reminded me so much of Karl's yacht, *Yoldia*. Except *Yacare* was two feet shorter (25 feet) and actually had a toilet. *Yacare* was French and the crew included Raphael, a software developer from Normandy, and Cocotino, a sprouting coconut that had now become a tree. With myself, a South-African-born, vagabonding gypsy with an allergy to shoes, and my giant teddy bear, Teddy, we were quite an eclectic crew.

Yacare was buddy-boating with another French boat, *Gamine*, who was a little larger and faster. But Jacques, the skipper from Britany, France, was up for an adventure and in no hurry to get anywhere.

It was Friday night and seeing as you should never set sail on a

Friday[3], we were sat at one of the tiny marinas enjoying a feast of Fijian food with a mix of salty sailors from the far reaches of the globe. I started chatting to a Swiss-Austrian who had been working hard to get a boat ready and was frustrated with the delays. By the end of the evening, Manu had joined Jacques' crew and a couple of days later we all checked out of Fiji and started our way toward the Solomon Islands.

I didn't know much about the Solomons, the only thing I'd read on the country said this:

*"The Solomon Islands is a melting pot of various ethnicities, and they don't always get along. One group or another is always unhappy, and they don't mind expressing it with a **protest**, which often turns into a **riot**, which sparks **looting** and general **lawlessness**... Trouble brews quickly here.*

*Honiara is also the **crime** capital of The Solomons, and wealthy-looking visitors are often a target. Leave the expensive watches and expensive jewellery at home. Don't walk around the streets alone at night (best to go with a group or a guide), and give the early morning jog a miss.*

*If you do go out to a bar at night, be aware there'll always be a few locals who like to **fight** – there were **active head-hunters** on these islands until the 1930s, so they probably know how to handle themselves.*

*During the day **pickpocketing, bag snatching, mobile phone theft and general harassment are common.***

***Yachties Beware**! Foreign governments also warn their yacht-based citizens to take care in Honiara harbour where there have been reports of **criminals boarding yachts at night** and stealing valuables. They are usually **armed and are not deterred if confronted**. It's best to let them take what they want and live to tell the tale.*

...Swearing is a crime. It can lead to compensation claims or jail, or both.

Homosexual acts (by either sex) are illegal and penalties include jail sentences.

---

[3] Sailors have long held that setting sail on a Friday is bad luck. There is some belief that it is because it is the day that Christ was crucified. More likely though, sailors simply wanted to stick around port to enjoy the weekend and decided to create a superstition to match.

Bull, Hammerhead and Tiger sharks *are present throughout Solomon Islands' coastal waters. The timid Reef Shark is harmless, but, unless you know the difference, be wary of all sharks.*

About **50 people are killed every year by saltwater crocodiles**. *These are locals, well-acquainted with the ever-present danger. Unsuspecting tourists are well-advised to seek advice before entering unfamiliar waters and to be wary in any case.*

In and around Honiara, **uncontrolled dogs roam freely**, *often in packs. Tourists are advised to be cautious.*

World Nomads, Solomon Islands: Everything you Need to Know Before You Go continued about cyclones, earthquakes, volcanoes, and other weather anomalies before I remembered why I don't normally read up on countries before I visit them. At least I had a nice ten-day sail up from Fiji to masticate this information and prepare myself for what [mis]adventures lay ahead. I was sure the native crocs were going to love our inflatable kayak.

We arrived at night. A giant phosphorescent crocodile swam over to pilot us into Groscious Bay, Santa Cruz. The jungle buzzed around us as we celebrated our arrival with a bottle of red. In the still of the anchorage, my heart raced: Pirates... Malaria... Were we safe?

The morning brought schools of visitors in dug-out canoes. Half-naked. Red betel nut toothed. Wild! There was a mix of missionaries, fishermen and traders. You can trade for just about everything in the Solomons; one college we visited encourages their students to pay tuition in dried fruit or pigs.

As we jumped between the islands and their bays we got sucked into the beauty of the wild. Bleach-blond kids would either paddle over to greet us or stand on the shore enthusiastically waving. Sometimes we would paddle ashore to glares and unwelcoming machete-wielding stances. But, without fail, our friendly "hello" to the various onlookers would return toothless smiles and friendships would be struck in minutes.

Such was the love for the Hapi Isles, that one crew member opted to plant roots. We bid Cocotino, our resident coconut tree, farewell in a very moving, well-attended burial ceremony. He had long outgrown the ceiling of our little vessel.

UNEMPLOYMENT LOOKS BETTER WITH A TAN

In Santa Ana, the people still challenge each other in warrior fights where spears are flung at neighbouring tribes to prove hero status. There are often fatalities, but the heroes live on in legend and their bones are kept as sacred reminders for future generations. It's a wild world out there. A beautiful one.

Even the capital, Honiara, and its dusty betel-stained streets had something genuine and raw about it. The dogs didn't seem to bite, and neither did the people.

While Rafael and Jacques sat doing some work, Manu and I accepted the offer of a friendly local and explored the island by motorbike. It was difficult to imagine such a tropical paradise as a war scene. Some of the palm trees still held bullets in them. Most of the bays were snorkelling paradises for those interested in wrecked ships, planes and bombs.

❦

I met a female sailor! This may sound commonplace, but Sharna and I spotted each other from across a bar and the rest of the day was lost in conversation while not giving the rest of our respective crews a moment of our attention. Serious travellers are a rare breed, and female ones even more so! We only spent a day together, but we knew already that our paths would cross again. Her crew sailed off to explore more of the Solomon Islands while we veered off to Papua New Guinea.

❦

The wind stopped just outside the anchorage. Despite the head start, it didn't take long for *Gamine* to catch up. And while I slept, or at least tried to, they threw us a line and a towing procession ensued. We followed them all through the afternoon and into the sunset. We continued being towed through a prawn dinner[4]. And, because *Gamine* was doing all the work, we decided that we could both sleep. But our heads literally hit the pillows

---

[4] These had become commonplace aboard *Yacare*, only I wasn't quite sold on canned prawns. Anything fishy that is canned really is a bit fishy.

when Jaques radioed through to tell us that our lazy days were over, the wind had just woken up.

It was good to be moving again. It was sad to be saying goodbye to the Solomons, but nice to be moving forward. My phone beeped through its last messages and notifications, and then we were back in the middle of nowhere again. The waves started crashing over us from the side, pretending not to notice us. I closed up the companionway and was grateful for the chance to finish Rafael's birthday preparations, even if it was a battle to do anything.

The following day, I planned to cook up a celebratory breakfast, but it was far too rough. And, even though it was the captain's birthday, we were both so tired that we kept missing each other as one of us was always asleep. The day after, I felt so guilty that I forced myself to cook. And I did it in the manner that only seasick sailors know: I tried to make breakfast lying down. It was hard work and disgustingly hot inside, but we needed to eat and the rotting vegetables needed saving! I still look back at this as one of my most galliant (Valliant in the Galley) achievements!

The weather continued to either hit us with wild waves, small storms, or too much heat. But it was beautiful out there. And with everything, including my stomach being a bit too rough, I shall share with you the only thing I managed to produce on the crossing; a poem.

Deep Sea Diarrhoea
(The outpouring of my heart and stomach)

Ever tried to take a poo while the seas swarm around you?
Ever tried to take a shit when there's nowhere safe to perch or sit?
Ever tried to take a dump while the waves crash you with a thump?

It's too hard to cook – instant soup!
It's too hard to stand this far from land.

After a somewhat unhealthy diet, your insides decide to riot.

UNEMPLOYMENT LOOKS BETTER WITH A TAN

You somehow stumble to the loo, but the bowl bounces like a kangaroo.
You hold on tight and push with all your might.

OHHHHH! Deep sea diarrhoea!

- Adeena Gerding, 31 August 2016

Phosphorescent dolphins leapt through the air, glowing as the plankton shone and then dripped back down to the water. I was exhausted, but it felt like I was exactly where I was meant to be. So much beauty. So much power. So much love struck me.

I remembered why I did the stuff I did, why I let my body endure the torture. I suddenly became passionate about life again. I crawled into bed, renewed. This trip was no accident.

"As you walk and eat and travel, be where you are; otherwise, you will miss most of your life"

- Buddha

5

Trading Bras for Pumpkins

"*Are you an African?*"
"How did you know?"
"You look like one?"
"You have met many?"
"No, I have never met an African."
I smiled in confusion
"But I have read about them. They are good people."

Charles was clearly incredibly wise and insightful so we carried on talking. We talked about good people. We talked about bad people (Papua New Guinea is renowned for their rascals - the raping, pillaging, lawless anarchists hungry to inflict pain and violence in their wake). We got talking about cannibals:

"The headman would choose who he would like to eat first. Sometimes the men. Sometimes the women. Normally visitors - especially the lumolumo" (*white men*; maybe I was tanned enough to avoid the palate?).

"And how would they eat them?"

"Well, first they would remove the head. The body would be cooked on a fire and served to the village. When the flies stop sitting on the head then it is ready to be boiled and turned into a soup. The soup is a special delicacy."

"IS!!??" I asked in a mild panic. "What do you mean 'is'?"

"No no no," said Charles. "We do not eat humans anymore. Now we have enough meat."

I wondered how their "meat" supply was doing with the famine and drought they'd experienced just the previous year. I delved deeper into the technicalities and the history of the matter and probably shouldn't have. Just one bay over, there still sat a boat where all thirty [plus] passengers were dragged ashore and feasted upon.

"And how long ago was that?"

"Ahhhh, not so long ago... maybe 40 years."

Raymond! Such a breath of fresh air. He arrived while I was doing the laundry.

"You can do your laundry over by that side in the waterfall," he said, pointing off into the vague distance.

"But you have motor dinghy?"

I shook my head and nodded at the inflatable kayak.

"Then no can. Crocodiles in river will eat you."

He smiled as he said it.

"220 people live in that village," he said while pointing ashore.

"Do they like yachties?" I asked.

"Yes, some."

"And the others?"

He never answered, he just made us sign his yacht book and then headed over to *Gamine*.

"She's half school[5]" chuckled the toothless betel nut chewers who'd tied up to our boat to give us yams as another waka outrigger paddled over.

We seemed to have an endless supply of curious visitors wandering over. Sometimes we'd still be dropping anchor when the friendly smiles would bargain and trade and want. Day. Night. Too frequently before morning coffee.

With only one supply boat visiting a year and maybe six yachts, some islands really were cut off from the outside world.

I traded three balloons for two coconuts and a bunch of tasty leaves.

I traded an old T-shirt for a bunch of bananas.

I traded beads or pens or notebooks for papayas.

Soap for wild bird eggs.

Fish hooks for potatoes.

Balloons were the first niche that all the kids wanted. In the next bay, it was bracelets.

Finally, I dug deep into my scant bundle of life belongings and produced luminous hair pins - they were an instant success.

We had more fresh supplies than we could eat!

I liked their way of life. Out there, money was about as useless as a roll of toilet paper that had been swimming in the bog.

"Can you help me please; I have cut my finger"

John climbed on board and removed his grass bandage. It didn't look like much, it was not infected and had already closed. We took out the first aid kit and disinfected it before covering it up with a "white men Band-Aid". We told him he'd live.

"And where are my pills?"

"Pain killers?"

"Yes. I need painkillers."

The first visitor the next morning needed the same thing. She claimed neck pain.

"Please miss, we are very remote."

Remote? Do "remote" people NEED lumolumo painkillers to

---

[5] One coconut short of a palm.

survive minor pains? Aren't these the wildest of the wild- people who wrestle crocs and horde off rascals? Aren't these people genetically fearless warriors?

I said a firm "No!" And almost added a "Flip off."

She paddled away miraculously appearing to be healed.

While it wasn't everywhere, there were some islands where visiting yachts had overtraded and introduced people to things they were never meant to be introduced to. When people "needed" yeast or water containers, it was normally for homebrew.

When we tried to give them swimming goggles, they simply spat them back in our faces and demanded our personal dive masks instead.

Boats coming from Australia would load up with bags of donated clothes and equipment for trading, so it was hard to communicate that the T-shirt I was trading had sentimental value and was one of the only four I owned...

We didn't hang around those places for long. The residents there seemed to forget about what was important in life!

We tried to stick to the places where we were welcomed and accepted. The places where waka sailors laughed as they breezed past and the smiles sang as they paddled home from their farms. Where the children simply wanted to give and smile and visit and play with your hair. Places where the community still held.

༺

"Are there crocodiles here?" I asked the smiling faces who'd paddled over to greet us as we arrived after a very rough passage.

"Yes! Plenty."

"In this bay?"

Synchronized nods.

"And do they attack?"

"Yes." [matter-of-factly as if to say "duh!"]

"Have you seen it?"

"Many times."

"And what about in your waka? Can they jump up and pull you down?"

"Yes. Can!"

I sensed that maybe we drew so many visitors because they wanted to give us food to fatten us up and make us more attractive to the neighbourhood pets. So much for swimming.

It was two days later on a lonely dusk [inflatable kayak] paddle back from the village that I stumbled upon a big shape drifting through the water towards me. It dropped down leaving two eye-like blobs submerged and then it vanished altogether. I cannot confirm the nature of the creature but it separated me from the yacht and left me at a bit of a quibble. Did I paddle faster and [hopefully] get back quicker? Or did I slow right down and drift in the current and wind hopefully to be mistaken as a log?

As you may have suspected I did make it back alive. The swarm of visitors all confirmed the nature of the creature to be as I suspected. They leave the rivers in the dry season in search of food and only return when sated. I was glad to be home - but I saw the anguish on the faces of our local guests who had a long dark row back in their dainty serving dishes.

As we hopped between beautiful islands and bays, I was continually challenged to face the fears that nature threw at me. I was in some of the most bewitching, unexplored islands on earth and I was towering in fear - almost too scared to enjoy them.

The crocodiles, sharks, malarial mosquitoes, pirates and cannibalism seemed to merely mirror the inner insecurities I needed to tackle. Fear of failure, fear of inadequacy, fear of disappointing others... These terrified me even more than the salties! It's amazing how much you learn about yourself when you completely remove all technological and worldly distractions and put yourself face-to-face with the elements.

As I began wrestling with self-issues, I found the natural threats becoming less alarming too. I began swimming and snorkelling the Pacific blues (when the kayak broke it became a necessity). I started exploring more and climbing the hills where "wild people" might reside. I got myself tangled in webs and had massive tarantulas crawl over me. I ran into a few huge sharks and got plenty of mosquito bites, but I began to trust that I'd be okay. After all, I also only had one chance to explore these almost untouched lands.

It took a long time to overcome my inner turmoil but If I could trade my bra for a pumpkin, I could trade in my insecurities for an unrestrained life.

I did. I think that one was a fair trade.

Life at Sea

Be all you can be.
Do. Go. Get around. See.
Chase happiness and dreams.
Ride rollercoasters and seas.
Live like there is no tomorrow,
A life of joy instead of sorrow.
Throw away your inhibition
Step into your life's mission.
Leave a [good] footprint on the earth.
The true purpose of your birth.

6

27⁰ Short

"***I want to go home.***"
It was weird to suddenly know what I wanted or almost needed. I was ready for community again. I wanted to stop aimlessly circling the planet and start what some people call "real life." And this time it was not for anyone else, it was for me. I was not chasing a boy or what society told me I should be doing. I was following an instinct that had merged with my gut. I was listening to myself for a change.

Port Moresby was allegedly the most dangerous city in the world. It was also where I decided to leave *Yacare*. When I broke it to Raphael that I would be disembarking, he panicked and retorted that he would be leaving first thing in the morning. He hoped I would not have the bravery to tackle the vicious city on my own and that I would stay on board. It was a rare occasion where I was decisive. I hugged him farewell and wished him travelling mercies. I prayed that I had made the right decision. I was only one week away from completing my circumnavigation. But suddenly, that didn't matter to me anymore.

When you take the steps you feel you need to take, no matter how big, small or ludicrous they may seem, you find exactly what you need. And on a jog that evening I literally ran into Craig. He was a friendly Aussie who had a boat in the marina. When I asked him about hostels, he laughed.

"No mate, you use my boat. It's wasting away with nobody aboard. There's just one condition though, you need to use Martha too. Stay as long as you like."

Craig was a saint. Martha was his delightful cleaning lady. He paid her to keep the boat clean, but she was going mad because the boat was never visited or used, so it never got dirty. Every stain in the scarce supply of clothing I had not traded was magically removed by Martha, who very quickly became both a friend and a drinking buddy.

I tried to find cargo ships heading for South Africa. I tried relocation cruises. But I didn't need more adventures. I decided to simply break with gypsy traditions and fly. "Simply" is a slight understatement though. It still took five flights.

Teddy got invited to sit in the cockpit on the way to Cairns, Australia. The captain swears he let the bear steer the plane. Then it was off to Bali where I took a week's breather. It had been three years since I had last visited my homelands and I needed to take stock of my life before returning. There's something both beautiful and unsettling about going home. It's amazing to reconnect with familiar beats and smiles. But every time I return a different person, a person who has grown and transformed. When you try and fit your new shape into the puzzle it used to fit into, there is normally some discomfort as you either completely reorganize the puzzle, or digress to put your old shoes back on. I'd given up on shoes completely.

Manu taught me to make an inverse bucket list, so I sat in my little slice of paradise writing out the things I had accomplished and learned since I had last set foot on African soil. My Airbnb turned out to be an Ashram, so I had many more lessons to learn before heading home. Despite being programmed against them as a child, I found value in yoga and meditation. Speaking to a resident artist helped me realise that I had spent so much time trying to carry other people and their problems, that I didn't give them space to learn how to deal with things themselves. The revelation hit me like a brick.

I spent a day in Bangkok buying gifts for friends and family back home and restocking my wardrobe. Seeing that I was a new person, some new clothes were probably in order. As seems to always be the case in Bangkok, my flight home could not be reserved online, so I found the back-alley travel guy I knew from years earlier. I trusted him with my logistics while I sat down to write a blog.

Home
Blog published October 3, 2016

In the last Nine years of Part-Time Professional Gypsyism (PTPG), this is the first time I've decided to go home for me.
Not for a wedding. Or by accident. Or for any other reason.
Just because it's time.
It's where I need and want to be.
I always thought I'd return fit and lean, with excessive bundles of foreign cash…
Instead, I carry a squiggly sailor's build and I'm broke (but fortunately not broken).
But if you wait for perfect conditions, you'd better be quite good at knitting.
I can't knit!
I'm not sure how long I'll be back for.
I'm not at all sure of the practicalities of what I'm setting out to do…
(The "epiphany" still carries some haziness)
For so long I have taken solace in knowing that I'm a good gypsy.
I'm good at scumming it; scavenging for food, hitching, exchanging skills and muscle for shelter and adventure.
I'm used to migrating. To moving. To letting life distract me.
But I crave a base. A home. Community.
I might be 27 degrees short of a circumnavigation, but for now I've had enough of licking foreign soils.

UNEMPLOYMENT LOOKS BETTER WITH A TAN

Enough stories.
Enough challenges and new places.
(For a while at least.)
It's time for something different.
It's time to catch up and reconnect with old friends (if any of you remember me?)
It's time to remember my roots.
It's very much time to get to the airport.
It's time to go home!

᠅

The flight would have been quiet and comfortable had another airline not cancelled their flight at the last minute. Every seat was filled and, much like a sinking ship, there seemed to be some sort of woman and children first principle in play.

In Zombie state, I stumbled about Ethiopia as I loaded up on coffee and spice and some other things nice. I tried not to think about the mad adventure I was about to embark on. After sailing and cycling and hitchhiking around the world, settling down felt like the scariest adventure imaginable!

᠅

Diary entry, 5 October 2016

The last time I left Addis, I was almost in tears. I didn't want to go home. Today I'm the happiest person in the world. I was about to sit down and take my seat when someone behind me yelled out, "Excuse me, aren't you Jeandre's sister?"

What are the chances of a friend's dad recognising me? Now I know that I'll be okay! Maybe I still do have a lot of people that I remember from my homelands. It hasn't sunk in yet, but some awesomeness lies ahead for sure!

Oh crap, it's only four hours and 30 minutes - it's too soon! I suppose it's too late to turn around now... I'm sitting here listening to Sigur

Ros and imagining the trip again. It's been epic. Even the bad (in retrospect) has been so good. How has it been three years already since I left? How come I'm this afraid? I've been through so much: pirates, heartbreaks, the Panama Canal, faith, hope and trust as I thought I'd die on the way to the Marquesas. Brokeness and brokenness. I've cycled across a continent and hitched in a onesie. I worked hard, played hard, and laughed hard. I've lost myself on boats and in oceans and cyclone-swept villages and I've kept rediscovering who I am.

I know I am a much stronger person than I used to be, but still, I'm terrified. There's so much unknownness that lies ahead. What state does the country lie in? What friendships and relationships lie ahead? What projects will my hands take up? How will I avoid homelessness? My mission intention[6] is written and I hope I manage to keep it and keep the goals in check. I hope I find the necessary distraction to keep me from boredom and from running away again.

How will I live out my calling? What adventures are to come?

Let the next chapter begin! Hopefully, it is even better than the last one! Home should be an even greater adventure than my travels!

The plane's ready for touchdown...

Hello South Africa, I'm ready for you.

I can't tell you how magically my arrival merged into a flow. From visiting my brother in the wild savannas where he was shooting wildlife documentaries. Then on to a friend's wedding that was taking place nearby. There just so happened to be a vacant caravan on the premises perfect for hosting my gypsy self on very short notice. Unfortunately, we had a childhood promise that the last to be married would have to pole dance at the other's wedding. The agreed-upon song was *Don't Cha* [wish your girlfriend...] by the Pussycat Dolls. It was very awkward, but it felt good to keep a promise.

My family all seemed to have time for reconnection. And friends too. I relished the North of the country and eventually set off for Cape

---

[6] My intention manifesto is included in the reference section of this book.

UNEMPLOYMENT LOOKS BETTER WITH A TAN

Town.

It was a Sunday and I sat at the table at my favourite restaurant with good friends and an average notepad. I already knew how many things I had missed out on in my years adrift and was tired of interrupting conversations to ask questions so I simply wrote down all the things I didn't know so that they could be researched later. *Tinder*, *Uber*, *CrossFit*... so many "new normals" had entered the world and I'd been left behind!

    A few dreams were crushed as I discovered that I was not allowed to live aboard a boat in the centre of Cape Town, but new dreams and passions were forming and there was enough to keep me moving forward in other aspects of life. My community started to build itself naturally. While many old friends had left Cape Town, some had relocated to Cape Town from different regions of the country. People I met while travelling lived just around the corner. I kept meeting the right people at the right time and I felt very much at home. I began writing down my travel stories because I felt like I needed to share them, to remind people to take risks and trust and get out of their comfort zones.

    And, to refamiliarize myself with my land, I took a job as a location scout for production companies. What better way to properly get to know your home environment than by exploring its rooftops, offices, tennis courts, fields, and bridges?

𓂀

Five, four, three, two, one... 2017 began. He looked at me and I looked at him. We both shrugged, smiled and pulled in to kiss each other. The bartenders cheered. Maybe it wasn't a good thing I knew them all. It was only a New Year's hook-up after all. I had never had one and I was all about trying new things. Or at least that is what it was meant to be. That was January, a month of confusion. A month spent either in the mountains or writing *"the book"*[7]. Sometimes writing *the book* in the mountains. A month of two boys because an ex had also re-entered my life and it was

---

[7] First We Ate Your Wife.

easier to say "yes" to both of them rather than "no" to either. The most excellent month of both guilt and pleasure. A month of pushing life to its ultimate limits: freedom, fitness, and fun. After all, life is what you make of it.

And then, all too quickly, February hit. February bought with it admission of guilt and sediments of responsibility. February bought with it the will to commit to something, to anything. It's funny how the Year of the Cock arrived and that's when I said goodbye to it. I didn't want to be a player. I can't, it's not who I am. In fact, instead of New Year's resolutions, I toyed with "Febalutions". I needed some goals and some purpose in my life, definitely more God. And so, the year and the adventure continued and I planned to spend much time in simple beauty and finally finish the infamous book I was writing. I planned to commit to church and friendship goals. I hoped to live epically and take the year to an even higher level of awesome. Lagom[8] was not an option.

"This will be "real life" and it will be an amazing adventure because that is the definition of real life."

I enjoyed music festivals and travelled my own country for fun, even giving hitchhiking a try. New friendships were born and new communities were having foundations laid.

On the 20th of April, a letter arrived that sent me stumbling in every direction. It changed all my plans and made me re-question everything. I called my bank in London straight away to check if I had the money I needed. I knew the account was blocked and had to be unblocked in person, but they couldn't even tell me if I still had an account with them or not. The next adventure was serious; it was all about stepping out in faith.

---

[8] The Swedish word for "Average." For them, "Lagom" is best.

UNEMPLOYMENT LOOKS BETTER WITH A TAN

ADEENA GERDING

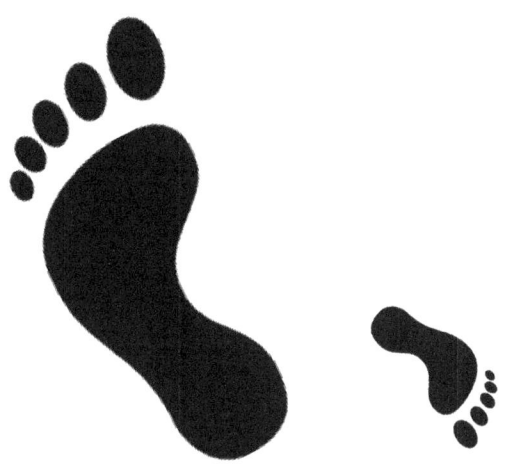

aNyWHeRe FoR a HuG.

UNEMPLOYMENT LOOKS BETTER WITH A TAN

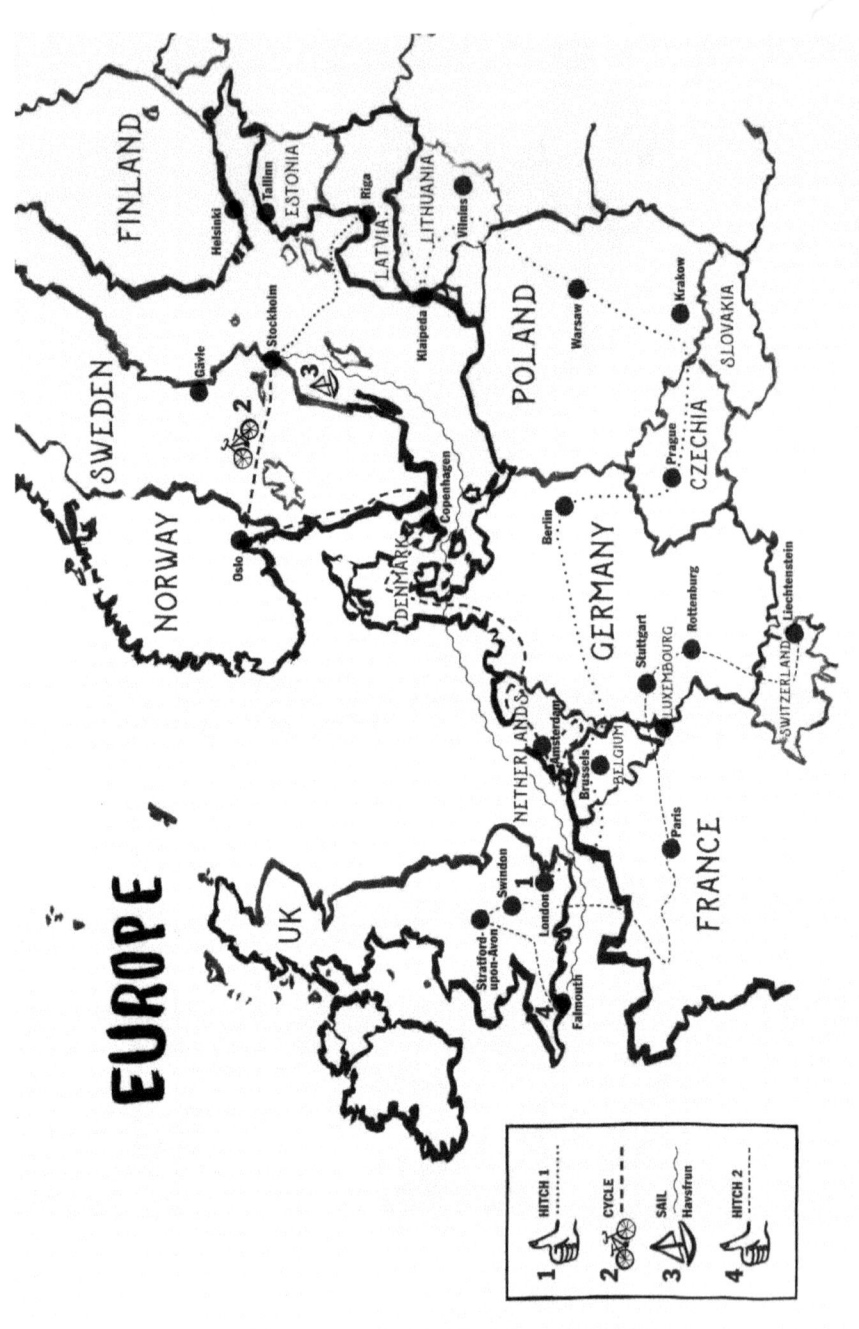

7

Refugee

When embarking on a mad adventure that you are unprepared for and petrified of, it is always good to start it with a hug and some smiling familiar faces. I decided to appease my troubled mind and call this chapter of my life "Anywhere for a Hug." And I meant it. A good hug, well applied, can bring even the most fearful gypsy back down to Earth.

It is also good to remember, before you get to the airport, that somewhere in your backpack is a bag of mushrooms someone had gifted you at Africa Burn. It is especially good to remember this when flying through Dubai. Good thing my Uber driver didn't mind pulling over for a minute. Now the big question was, was this a good time to try mushrooms for the first time?

𓂀

Megan was the reason I had moved to London in the first place. She had spent months organising visas and exploring job opportunities. I had simply spent an afternoon catching up with her in Johannesburg and a random series of events ensued that led me to purchase a flight ticket with her. We had jumped continents a decade earlier. While I had continued to loop around the globe, she had stayed put and even bought herself a little house. This was where my new adventure began, in good company and a safe space.

Many other friends had moved on or moved to more family-friendly cities now that they too were in new life chapters. It was a beautiful time of exploration and catching up with curious characters while trying to wrap my head around their new lives.

My bank fortunately still held the emergency funds that I had set aside years before but seeing as Brexit was on the cards and I was no longer a resident, I wasn't allowed to keep an account. They could give me all my money in cash, but was it a good idea to hitchhike with lots of money[9] on me? Was it a good idea to hitchhike when Europe was full of desperate refugees? Was it a good idea to hitchhike at all?

I was due to leave London early that Saturday morning. I hugged Megan goodbye at 5:30 a.m. when she set off to run a marathon. By ten, I was still freaking out about the journey that lay ahead of me. Of course, there were buses, trains and planes going my way, but where was the joy in that? Although it terrified me, I needed a real adventure.

I took a deep breath, said another prayer, picked up my backpack and my teddy bear and walked down the stairs. I paused, threw in the keys, and the door locked behind me. I still had a bit of credit left on my Oyster Card, so I simply hopped on board the bus that had just pulled up outside. I didn't care where I was going. When the bus started veering in the wrong direction, I pinged the button and hopped off. I crossed a park that turned out to be a golf course and, after dodging golf balls and enduring sufficient laughs, I stuck out my thumb. And so began the hitch to watch a friend get hitched. I had six days to get to the Czech Republic.

---

[9] By Gypsy standards.

The first car stopped. It was so unexpected that I wasn't ready for it. The family filled me with hope for the journey ahead, even if five-year-old Sophie wanted all her cats to die so that she could get bunnies.

The M25 was a bit too busy for my liking. When my bra came undone and I tried to fix it without removing my backpack, I got offers for anything but what I was looking for, a nice friendly ride to Dover.

A lot of hoots, zaps, yells, kisses, and offers in the wrong direction later; a car finally stopped. The Albanian wasn't going very far, but I was very happy to simply have a change of scenery. He had been in London for 17 years and missed his family immensely. As we discussed the hardships of him being away from his wife and two kids, it emerged that he was indeed hoping to have sex with me. I used to panic in these situations, but fortunately that day I had my head screwed on firmly and managed to steer the conversation towards commitment and vows and what that meant. We got so deep into conversation that he ended up driving me all the way to Folkstone where we continued the discussion over a beer. I am pretty sure that he left knowing that he needed to change. I left knowing I needed to meet him.

A Welshman dropped me off at the ferry and instead of entering the ticket office, I thought I would take a different approach and see if I could get a free ride. I stuck out my thumb and made a sign that said "Ride onto ferry". It took a while and I got a lot of laughs, but a man towing a bulldozer rolled down his window.

"You must be very lazy," he said with a smile.

"I'm just trying to see if it will work," I replied as I hopped in.

"I picked up a hitchhiker so there are two of us now," he said to the ticket administrator.

She checked our passports and waved us in without any additional costs. Sam was in awe.

It was a painfully awkward conversation as we sat waiting for the ferry. When the conversation ran completely dry, he turned on the American Cup. Finally we had sailing in common. From then on, we were mates. He made me coffee, and I treated him to a beer on the ferry. And when we arrived in Calais, we disembarked together with him dropping me off just outside the city with a hug.

I strolled the canal eyeing out potential camp spots and pausing to eat a can of curry beans to lighten my load. I was finally back in Europe, in France. Every country should begin with a beer so I continued walking to where I supposed a bar would be. But the night had other plans.

"You need place to stay?" Asked a smiling man.

I guess I had been asking God for a place to stay, but could I trust this man? He spoke very little English and I didn't have any French, but I ascertained the gist of his goodness and followed him. Sometimes all we have to go on is our guts. But no matter the situation, it is always good to be on an adventure with God because there is no better person to have your back!

And He does have a seriously good sense of humour. Unbeknownst to me, I was facing one of my biggest fears already. My new friend was an Afghani refugee. I spent the night sitting up with him and his friends discussing travel. Only, what they did for survival, I did for fun! We shared Ramadan breakfast just before sunrise at which point, I finally went to sleep.

I bid them farewell a few hours later and found a little café where I sat sipping away while trying to catch my mind up with my body by scribbling in my travel diary. I tried to pay, but the café didn't accept cards, Pounds or South African Rands. I got my coffee for free. It was my third free coffee since leaving my homelands, and I was beginning to think it was some kind of joke. My church group had gifted me a "Cappuccino Fund" because they knew the importance of coffee in my life. I had planned to send them a thank you when I finally touched it, but I hadn't had the opportunity yet.

It was a long wait until I got my first ride. It was only a short trip, but a few kilometres can put you in a much better spot. I thanked the Moroccan and hopped in with two French ladies. I wasn't sure where they were heading, but they laughed a lot, so I did too! I wound up in Dunkirk, Belgium, where they resupplied their cigarette stash and headed back.

I held out a Bruges sign, but Sophie assured me that Ghent was much nicer. She could have told me anything and I would have believed her, so strong was the air of goodness she carried! Before I knew it, I had agreed to stop off in Dikkelvenne first to join her for an art tour by bicycle.

A colourful group of people had assembled at her mother's house. Somebody loaned me a bike and we raced off through the neighbouring villages where many people had opened their homes to display incredible art pieces and sculptures. Good food, Great company, and beer! I got a whole lot more than I had bargained for! And at the end of it all, Sophie dropped me at her friend's house in Ghent. Els was another beautiful soul that I needed to meet.

After a morning skinny dip and coffee, she was late. As an air hostess, it's even more important that you make your flight on time! While she had offered me a lift to Brussels, we both agreed it was better to explore Ghent first. And I am glad I did, not only was it beautiful, but there were more people that I needed to meet.

Ilse[10] and Miguel were just getting to know each other when I met them in Laos in 2009. Now they have two beautiful children. The reconnection took me 36 km backwards from where I was headed. But the kids won my heart and their parents won the appreciation of my liver with their beer aperitifs.

Ilse was sick, but after throwing up, she still made me coffee before Miguel dropped the kids at school and me at the petrol station. It was pouring with rain and freezing cold, but I still had my intuition in check and turned down the first ride I was offered. Everything in my stomach churned as I chatted to the driver. I felt almost suffocated and could only breathe again once I had watched them drive out of sight. A few people came to say hi, but it took forever to get a ride actually heading in the right direction. The Windmill technician, a father of three (all born exactly a year apart) dropped me on the outskirts of Antwerp where it didn't take long to find another ride.

My new driver had just started a business teaching people to make decisions based on feelings rather than logic. Some bad life turns had landed him in debt and thrown him out of Canada without him even having had the opportunity to meet his son. But despite the two accidents that stretched our short drive long, he was now very much on the right path! I bought him lunch, and as if God were still laughing at me, he bought me coffee.

I didn't even have my thumb out when I got my next ride, all the way to

---

[10] She was also my first ever passenger, on my first ever day driving my first motorbike. I'm glad we survived so we could become friends!

Köln. It felt weird passing through the Netherlands without stopping. It was my fatherland and my second citizenship, but I had never actually been there. A short visit would not do it justice though. Yes, according to my definition, a visit to a country must contain a minimum of one beer and a wee, but when it comes to heritage, there is so much more. What exactly? I had no idea, but I was excited to find out.

Instead, I spent the night in Köln. Similar to Berlin, I was once more surprised by the un-Germanness of the city. Halfway across the love-locked Hohenzollern bridge, I and my new Iranian best friend paused to write and throw off a message in a bottle. We had known each other all of seven minutes. When you are on the right path, good things seem to flow from everywhere and culminate in long picturesque sunsets on the Rhine and last rounds at the hostel bar.

I got stuck in the rain plenty of times the following day, but every time I did, I seemed to meet someone of awesome proportions who out-shadowed the shower. An American gave me a ride and went out of her way to show me Wuppertal where I pretended to be impressed by the upside-down train. She later dropped me off on the autobahn. Here the cops picked me up. They checked my passport and drove me 120m. The woman pointed at the ground and said "Autobahn." And then she pointed at the ground where we stood and said: "No autobahn" with a smile. It was much safer, but it was also the worst spot ever, there was absolutely no traffic. I walked into town and when the rains plummeted down, I found a small fuel station where I finally bought myself a coffee. The teller made for excellent company and restored my soul and my teddy bear by gifting him a nice plastic bag of protection. Another customer gave me a ride to the next fuel station where I waited for so long that I prepared to spend the night.

A fancy Audi pulled up from nowhere and offered me a ride to Berlin. He was chasing down his girlfriend who had stormed out of the house a few days earlier. Excellent company, but a crazy driver. He had far too much faith in the autosteer on his vehicle. Do you know that in Germany the word "expert" is allegedly not reserved for experts? The youngster had labelled himself a diamond "expert" and had been making a killing ever since.

I was dropped off on the outskirts of town. I started walking, but when a bus rocked up with the rain, I decided to take it. The driver let me ride for free and made someone else responsible for showing me where to get off to find a cheap hostel. I still got lost, but I am pretty sure I ended up exactly where I was meant to be. Berlin was the first European city I had ever fallen in love with.

What I didn't love about it was getting out! Eventually, a caring soul went out of his way to get me to a fuel stop on the autobahn. Here I met Jacob, a 19-year-old Dane who was also hitchhiking. He was on his way to a music festival. We were still discussing combining forces when a car pulled up and the 33-year-old German gifted us not only a ride but coffee and much wisdom from his own hitchhikes through Europe. We said our goodbye to him near the border and waited. It was getting dark and still, we waited. Jacob was even worse at sitting still than I was. He disappeared for a while and returned beaming. We had a ride to Prague!

We squished into the car and bounced our way across the border as the sun set and the moon rose and we sang and shared stories. They hot-spotted me so I could make plans for my arrival. Lukas assured me that *The Cross Club* was the best night spot in the city. With the welcome party that I received, I very much believed him!

UNEMPLOYMENT LOOKS BETTER WITH A TAN

8

Confusion and Vodka

As *we swam for our lives,* we swore that, if we survived, we would attend each other's weddings someday. At that point, marriage was as far off our horizon as the distant island that we swam for. But there she was, standing in front of me on her second to last day as a single woman, Helena. Some people stay the same no matter how many years pass between hugs.

Her wedding lasted two days and they were two awesome days of confusion and vodka. I knew nobody, but I didn't have a chance to be lonely! Helena's family took it in turns thanking me for saving her life, and I didn't have the opportunity to profess that I was the one who put her in danger in the first place. The only Czech I knew was "Na zdraví[11]" and "Alenka v říši divů[12]" (which was much less useful).

All the celebrating had me in the mood for more celebrations and, if I remembered correctly, Midsummer was just around the corner. I know that every country has its own way of celebrating Midsummer, but I wanted to experience the Swedish penis pole and the frogs with no tails first-hand. I had many friends in Sweden, but I thought I would ask Karl first, seeing as it was Karl who had taught me all about the customs. And it was Karl I had last risked my life with. And it was Karl that I most wanted to see. I was nervous, but I was now habituated to facing my fears. He answered immediately with, "Yes! Come!"

So, I left one massive festival on the quest for the next!

It took six hours and three different hitchhiking spots to get out of Prague. Normally the best rides are worth the wait. There are days when you seem to be invisible until God spotlights you to the right passerby. Nobody understands how God works and some days it seems like He is just having fun. We should do likewise, even if we don't quite understand His workings.

I woke up outside Ikea. The friendly Hungarian-Romanian driver had kindly offered me a seat in his van, to crash in after we'd stayed up late sipping beer and discussing life. Life brings about many discussions and I think I may never tire of contemplating and sharing other's views on it. And I know I will never stop learning from it. I'd slept well even if my drifting off had been interrupted with, "Do you want to have sex?"

"No, thank you."

"Okay, that's alright."

I hiked through fields of flowers and deer to get to the road to Ostrava. The traffic was frightful, but it worked to my advantage as a friendly local picked me up fearing for my survival. He left me with good vibes and two beers (one for me and one for Teddy). I hadn't even finished packing them away when a truck motioned for me to get in. I was carefully contemplating a nap on the soft grass where he left me, but some strangers

---

[11] Cheers.

[12] Alice in Wonderland.

came over to give me a motivational talk about going the distance. So, I pulled myself together and stuck out my thumb once more. Almost immediately another door opened and a friendly smile drove in the wrong direction just so that he would have the honour of driving me across the border.

Poland! I wasn't ready for it. I didn't expect Eastern Europeans to be so welcoming and friendly. And while my sign read "Krakow", it took only five minutes before I was in a truck heading for Warsaw. The driver's eyes sparkled as he told me about his son and wife and how much he loved them. He was always happy to go back to Bosnia to see them, but he had never taken them with him because he was afraid that they would be jealous and always have to drive with him. Normally my new friend would watch three movies with subtitles as he drove, but he was really happy to have human company for a change. Truck drivers have a very different window on the world. It was great conversation taking in his view on society, as well as discussing his favourite lunch spots all through Europe.

35 km out of Warsaw, I was dropped off at a fuel station. It was getting cold, so I paused to dig out warmer clothes. When I looked up, a car was waiting and I was told to get in. The driver spoke no English, but I was about to have my mind blown by the audible version of *Google Translate*. My noble knight gave me a full tour of the city before dropping me at a hostel. God really was smiling down on me as the receptionist checked me in. They were not allowed to accept walk-ins after nine p.m., but her replacement was an hour late and she felt like breaking the rules. The snoring in the dorm made me less grateful, but it did get me up for a morning run.

I loved the beauty of the derelict ruins of the old city. I loved the smells that lingered in the brisk grey morning fog. The Soviet style. The uniformity in people's dark dress and darker smiles. There is something magical in misery. There is also something mysterious about Polish washing machines. The closest laundromat was allegedly a bus and a tram ride away. The confusion this caused found me a new friend, and I allowed Mirek (a lawyer by trade, a life-lover by nature) to make my plans for me. I followed him to a nicer, cheaper hostel with a washing machine and was introduced to budget-friendly cuisine and the local community workspace. For the first time in years, I sat down to edit a video about my adventures.

UNEMPLOYMENT LOOKS BETTER WITH A TAN

It was hard to leave Warsaw, it held something captivating that made me want to linger. After multiple cups of coffee, a catholic procession, and many hugs, I finally bid my new friends goodbye. I hiked to the outskirts of town where two people who had not seen each other in years both stopped simultaneously to offer me lifts.

My next ride was busy explaining how the speed limit worked on the different road systems in the country when the police pulled her over for speeding. Luckily, she was in good spirits and we had even the policeman laughing as he issued her the fine. They dropped me at what they thought was a fuel station but was really a 24-hour bar. Poland.

I got lost in the heart of Bialystok and became an Instagram craze amongst the youngsters who helped me find my way back on track. They were wrong, and someone stopped to tell me and drive me to a better spot. He returned ten minutes later because he found an even better spot for me. I planned to set up camp there because it was so lush and beautiful and I was tired. But a car pulled up.

"Are you a hitchhiker?" they asked, looking hopeful.

I couldn't disappoint. The boot was broken and they already had four people in the car, but they made room for me and my many belongings and thrust the bear on their laps and a beer in my hand.

"Welcome to the party," they said and turned the music up.

"We are on our way to a concert, do you want to join?" yelled the driver.

I quickly downed my second beer as we entered the alcohol-free concert where I had a chain of people constantly holding my hands to not lose me in the thousands of dancers. All my worldly belongings were in their car and I didn't have a SIM card in my phone. The Polish can dance, I had no option but to join the celebrations! They knew everybody and I felt lucky to know them. After hugs, I walked in the direction they pointed me in and I pitched my tent.

It's strange waking up when you have no idea where you are or what the world looks like outside your tent. I felt the rocks and brambles sticking through my groundsheet and questioned how I had rested so well. The sizzling warmth of my little tent made it necessary to move and I unzipped myself to the outside world: a billboard and a field. Perfect. People buzzed around me, but nobody seemed to care. I sipped my morning coffee breathing in the epicness of life.

My toothbrush was missing, so I ducked into Tesco for a new one and spent my last four zloty on an ice-cream while I used the Wi-Fi to Skype Ouma. Grandmothers definitely lift your spirits and make your heart smile that little bit larger! Especially mine.

The sky spat amorously upon me as I walked towards the road to hitch, but it was the right time to leave, I felt it! I stood at the turnoff half committed while still questioning running for shelter when two hearty women took me in. They were heading to Lithuania to buy cattle. The perfect end to Poland. And being dropped right on the border was a new beginning too. I smiled and sang out loud as I lifted my thumb. There was no way this adventure could get any better.

And then it rained, or actually poured. A car passed and I pleaded. Nothing. Another sped by. One stopped, waited till I was a step away, and sped off laughing. And then the rain stopped too. I put my bags down because they were getting too heavy. I waited again. The flowers were beautiful. The clouds danced through the vast sky exploding in strange shades of grey. Another car. I smiled after it. A little more rain and no more traffic. And then that car returned.

"I had to pick you up for some reason," said the amazing smile of a man.

"Thank you! I'm Adeena," I grinned.

"Andrius," he replied with a hug.

We played car Tetris trying to make space for me. Andrius had just driven back from London and had his whole life in the car. He was also late for a dentist appointment, making his stopping even more meaningful. Kaunas arrived all too quickly.

"Look, I have to go straight to a dentist appointment, but if you are happy to wait a little, you are welcome to stay at my mom's house tonight. She's busy cooking all my favourite dishes to welcome me home."

How could I possibly turn down such an offer? It got better too, when he discovered that I was a sailor, he offered to drive me to the coast because he was starting a sailing course in the morning.

Lithuanian food is delicious! And Andrius's mum was delightful. I didn't even feel like I was crashing a family reunion, I felt at home; like I belonged. He never told his mother I was coming, he wanted to surprise her. She thought I was crazy with no shoes and no plan, but I think she liked me regardless! There was so much food that I faded off into a food coma on the couch. I was excited to be in yet another new country and thanked God for blowing my mind with His awesomeness.

I managed to hitch a ride out with the sailing school when I got to Klaipeda. And I was happy to teach the first timers the ropes as we slipped out of the dock, fuelled, and crossed the bay. I had no idea what to do on the Coronation Split, but I stuck out my thumb and wound my way to the campsite Andrius had recommended. I pitched my tent, left my bags and wandered off to find the beach. Unfortunately, I have no sense of direction, so I ended up at the Russian border instead. "Hmmm, what to do? Should I…?" I was carrying both my passports for safekeeping and I knew that South Africans no longer required visas for Russia. Why not cross the border for a beer?

The Lithuanians let me out, but I wasn't allowed to cross the border on foot. I hitchhiked the 30 metres across no man's land. I had no idea what a burden such a short hitch could be. There was no English. Border Control could not understand why I did not have a visa. They would not comprehend that I simply wanted to cross the border for a beer. A translator was called. My poor hitchhiker family waited. And waited. And eventually, I convinced the border control military to let them go. Two hours was long enough for people I simply wanted a short ride from.

The translator wasn't much help and I was held in a room by a host of armed military personnel while a new translator was found. Nobody cracked a smile and I couldn't take it any longer. I was very thirsty; I just wanted a beer. I tried to make this clear. One of them took a chance to believe he understood what I wanted.

"Nobody comes to Russia for the beer," he said.

"Except me."

And minutes later they could not keep the smiles from their faces any longer and they all burst out laughing. By the time the General and a real translator arrived, there were stitches in everyone's stomachs. They opened up the duty-free shop, let me buy my beers and watched me drink one. I had to down the last half because a bus was passing by and they put me on it and sent me straight back to Lithuania. I know that they were sad to see me go.

The split was incredible and the beach, when I did find it, was really pretty. I cracked open another beer and was disappointed to find it was alcohol-free. Life is full of surprises.

The stars sparkled and life was rather beautiful in the little corner of paradise. I met hordes of wonderful people to laugh and eat with and had a morning of swims and giggles. When I checked out of the campsite, I saw the Wi-Fi sign and connected. Andrius: He had given up on his sailing course and was coming to find me.

When I reached the sand dune, we'd agreed to meet at, I found my tribe. Scores of colourful people were mulling about and my hippy pants attracted them like moths. After reuniting with Andrius and exploring, we followed them back to Klaipeda where they were running a bicycle workshop for kids. It sounded cool, but the reality of the workshop blew my mind. They had all the old Burning Man bicycles shipped to Lithuania where they were running a program for troubled kids, building their dream bikes: double story, trikes, tandems, and tourers. I am not in any way exaggerating; it was fully awesome!

Andrius dropped me off on the side of the road and we were still hugging each other goodbye when a car pulled up and offered me a ride. I supposedly couldn't leave Lithuania without seeing the Hill of Crosses, so Gabrielius stopped so I could have my mind blown even further.

He dropped me off a few kilometres further down the road with a punnet of strawberries. It was almost ten p.m., but the sky was still alight, so I tried to push my luck and make it even further. And so it was that I crossed the border into Latvia and found a bush to call home for the night.

Only a couple of days remained until midsummer and some big route decisions had to be made. There was no way I could make it to Estonia and Finland, but there was a cheap ferry to Stockholm from Riga, so I headed that way with some amiable school teachers.

Hitchhiking was at its best and life was so good that I questioned whether I was actually alive or in Heaven. Even my dreams never flowed as perfectly as my life did then.

The ferry was comfortable and entertaining but I finally had time to think and wonder. I was excited to celebrate the festival, but I was even more excited to see Karl. He had been my best friend and favourite person. I knew nothing of what his current life looked like. He'd started university and we'd not spoken much over the past few months. Who was he then? What was his family like? I'd spoken to them so often, but I didn't have a clue who they were in person. Who were his friends? Was he single? Or did he have an awesome girlfriend? Was I ready to stumble back into his life?

9

Fuck.

The Swedish archipelago was astonishingly beautiful. I'd underestimated the time it took for the sun to sink and spent hours gazing in awe off the ferry. It dipped in the Baltic Sea and started rising again almost as soon as it set. And so did my insecurities. What was I stepping into?

I'd barely slept and hadn't spoken to the roommates I shared my cabin with.

"Why are you here?" asked a girl from the neighbouring bunk as I grabbed my bags.

"For midsummer," I replied nonchalantly.

She could see there was more to my story. She was meeting her boyfriend after a long time of being apart. I assured her that she looked beautiful. She told me I did too. I needed that. I also needed to share a hug with a stranger because my heart was screaming so loud, that I had to quiet it down somehow.

I breathed myself to calmness as the crowds slowly disembarked.

I was going to take it easy, get off the ferry, work out how to get into the city centre, and then find a coffee and Wi-Fi to ask Karl where to meet him. I didn't know where I would be sleeping, I did not know anything. The doors opened and the crowds poured down the gangplank. I saw his face immediately, smiling, handsome, ready. Suddenly I was in an embrace and I was home. I was safe. I was back.

We tried to catch up on each other's lives, but it had been too long, too much had happened. And none of it seemed to matter, only the present, his presence. The memories I had of our past were suddenly so strong. I hadn't realised how much he meant to me. I hadn't realised how much I had missed him. I followed him onto one subway and the next. Then into his exquisite apartment, he truly was living the High Life, even if it was borrowed from his aunt.

"I have a surprise for you," Karl had said earlier, almost bursting. But I still didn't know what it was. After a cup of coffee, I followed him again, as he smiled that Karlish grin. We were off to meet some of his friends but the bus ride was surprisingly long.

"Your friends live on a boat?" I asked as we finally disembarked and started towards a small jetty off the marina.

Karl just carried on smiling.

Jo and Oskar were pretty chilled, but they desperately needed help. Karl had spent the past week captaining their sail down from Gävle. They should have arrived already, but they'd had an engine failure and had to spend the night in Vaxholm. S/Y *Lydia* was a Vega too, but four feet smaller than *Yoldia* had been.

The boys had borrowed a replacement engine, but when they tried to swap the outboard engines, they sunk the stand they were trying to mount it on. There was a sense of déjà vu, reminiscent of our Pacific crossing, where Karl and I instinctively sprang into action to fix each challenge as it arose. After a rescue dive and a beer run, we got underway and set sail for Stockholm.

There are few things more beautiful than sailing into Stockholm in the setting sun, even if the new engine also failed and we were recklessly steering against the traffic with the aid of liquid courage. Manoeuvring the locks without an outboard was no joke, but Karl and I were used to navigating boating battles, we naturally functioned as a team.

We arrived much later than anticipated and were delayed further to savour celebratory champagne. We had to run to get back to Karl's to collect our belongings for midsummer. We just made the tube and took a deep breath for the few stops that led to his apartment.

"Shit!" Karl cursed.

"What is it, mate?"

"My girlfriend has the key."

It was the first mention of her and I didn't have time to think as we ran while he was on the phone to her. We had eight minutes to grab our stuff and get back in time for the last train. I briefly shook hands with her before we disappeared again and dove onto the train. Oskar had been prepared and held our seats, he was headed for Gävle too. We sat down and cracked open a celebratory beer, that's when the announcer told us we would be delayed.

We didn't have tickets and we weren't allowed to drink on the train, but my tipsy foreignerism talked us out of a fine for both and we somehow managed to keep drinking. Unfortunately, we missed our connecting train, but we found a spot to cuddle together for warmth while watching the not-so-subtle thieves try and steal bicycles from the lot in Uppsala.

"Should we try it?" asked Oskar in Swedish.

I didn't know we were breaking even more rules but followed them onto a train we undeniably weren't meant to be on.

"Biljetter," asked the lady doing the inspecting.

I gave her a blank look and asked for English.

"Tickets please."

"Well, we missed our connecting train because of the delays," I replied.

She seemed sympathetic and made sure we knew we weren't supposed to be drinking either.

"Really?" I asked, surprising myself with the character I had stepped into.

"When did you get to Sweden?"

"This morning," I smiled.

"Where are you heading?" she asked after welcoming us to Sweden.

"Gävle."

"Why Gävle?" she asked, honestly surprised.

The boys were shaking, they were holding their laughter back so hard. Somehow, we got away with it and somehow, we managed to tumble into Gävle, very drunk at 4:43 in the morning sun. We walked over to Karl's family home, made dinner and pestered Karl's brother, Martin, awake to join us.

"You can share my bed or take the couch," Karl said when we were finally ready to sleep.

I wanted nothing more than to wrap myself up in his warm arms, but I took the couch. It was the safer option.

I was up long before the others, so I made myself a cup of coffee and sat down to watch the magic that is a robotic lawnmower. Martin awoke next and I had a nice bonding session with him before we forced Karl out of bed, it was midsummer and we weren't going to miss it. After another cup of coffee, we walked through the streets of Gävle to catch the bus to Karl's father's house. Another long bus ride ensued because all I had been doing since arriving in Europe was transit.

Leif was exactly as I had imagined him, tall and calm and wise and funny. And his Irish girlfriend, Colette, carried the air of awesome I'd envisioned. I hugged them as if I had always known them. After meeting the rest of Ireland that she had visiting her, we got productive in constructing our tent and deconstructing beers. I found it funnier to watch in the end, the boys were clueless and the Irish commentary was very entertaining.

The instruments started emerging and people came out in their full midsummer swag as the "penis pole" had its last flowers added and the spread started to decorate the lawn. I felt like I was a Swede.

We raised the maypole and then our glasses of schnapps. We proceeded to throw around a plastic pig before we were summoned to the table. We feasted on meatballs and a smorgasbord of pickled herring as the songs belted out and my Swedish improved by the drink. And then we danced, like frogs with no tails, around "the penis." The band played; the laughter roared. We crawled into the tent at last.

"Can I cuddle you?" asked Karl.

I knew I could trust him, but did he trust himself? Closer closer.

So tight I would burst. He came inside. There was no way he couldn't; we couldn't break with Swedish tradition.

We could not look each other in the eyes in the morning. We had shared the most beautiful night but it wasn't right. He was not single. I was, but that didn't make me feel any less guilty.

After morning formalities like champagne and breakfast, we were back on the bus to get to the ferry to get to Karl's smultronställe[13]. A place I had heard so much about and dreamed of visiting. I napped for most of the bus ride and was in full form to meet up with more friends at the ferry dock. People I hadn't seen in years.

The Summerhouse was even nicer than I imagined it, perfectly adorned in a coat of natural flowers and good vibes. We feasted and played a plethora of games and climbed the lighthouse for sunset, which was also sunrise because in the height of summer in Northern Sweden, the sun never actually set.

That night we connected deeper than I ever have with anyone. The whole house shook as we did with our bodies what words would not allow us to speak. We belonged together, even if we could not acknowledge it. The same guilt darkened the morning and while we couldn't look each other in the eyes, we also couldn't allow our bodies to be apart. How had we suffocated all of these emotions for so many years?

We took the four p.m. ferry back to Gävle and were going to head straight back to Stockholm but Karl's mum, Inger, rang. She wanted to meet me too. I'm not sure what I was more afraid of, properly meeting Karl's girlfriend and finding out that she was awesome or having Inger greet me with a pitchfork. The first time I had spoken to Inger was when I had called from Panama to tell her that her son was in the hospital because I had burned his penis.

She was so lovely that I hugged her twice, once before and once after the shower. This was also to reassure her that I wasn't as smelly as

---

[13] **His favourite place.** It is (literally) a spot where (many) wild strawberries (Fragaria vesca) grow. (figuratively) a pleasant place with sentimental and personal value.

she first perceived.

"Skål för fan [14]," I said, raising my glass to cheers without thinking.

Everyone laughed, including his grandparents, aunt and cousin. It suddenly struck me that these were the people who would be reading my book. Karl hadn't told our story to anyone, including his friends. He'd forgotten most of it himself. It's a story he had hidden away because it was 'too much' somehow. Too complicated, too hard, far too intense. The lawnmower rudely interrupted our dinner and kept trying to knock itself out on the table, Inger put it to rest. I accidentally swore again in relief, it seemed my Swedish was of limited vocabulary.

Strangely enough, I had friends from my travels scattered all over Gävle. So many that I was convinced it was the second-largest city in Sweden. It is not, but it is the town most famous for its goat which gets burned every year at Christmas. What's not to like about a burning goat? Inger gave me a tour of the city before dropping us at the train station, it lasted all of 15 minutes.

We needed distraction on the train ride back, things were intense. So, we connected to the Wi-Fi to find out what had happened to *Yoldia*. Jonas had left her in the capable hands of… we weren't even sure where he had left her, but he had. He had other priorities now that he was a dad. And *Yoldia* now belonged to the *Sea-Star* hippies. Their blog seemed to suggest that they had bought the boat for $800. But from whom? And why was she now orange?

Karl interrupted, "Do you mind if I don't break up with her straight away?"

I was far away in the Pacific.

"What? How? No, of course not."

Flip! How was I going to deal with the two of them together? How was I going to be in the same house with them? My mind wanted to scream and cry and laugh. I wanted to run.

She met us at the train station. My worst fears were confirmed, she was lovely. I was a terrible person. We bought some beers and a picnic and

---

[14] Cheers for Fuck's sake.

they took me to their favourite rock for a stunning view of Stockholm. The drizzle dissolved into a rainbow.

"I told you so, Mate," said Karl while he stroked her back, "it's the most beautiful city in the world."

It was pretty, but I found it quite difficult to concentrate on the prettiness of the city when my whole life was playing out and escaping in front of my eyes. I wanted to do the same.

I spent the morning catching up with my friend Johan. We had met in Cambodia when we had had the same choice in footwear and similar difficulties with a hostel owner. I'd last seen him in Australia a few years earlier where he had run and given me a very unexpected hug and an even less expected campervan. Now he had two kids and a third due any day. As well as an incredible wife and a chain of sushi restaurants. It was a day to remember as we did menial tasks with maximum laughter. When the end of the day approached (even in Stockholm, nightfall was not a midsummer trend, there was still so much light) he offered me a bed to crash in and I accepted. I didn't want to go back to Karl's; I couldn't.

I connected to the Wi-Fi to tell him I'd be out. My phone wouldn't stop beeping with notifications, strange numbers… Karl's friends were individually telling me to come on over. They were throwing a party to meet me and I wasn't there! Karl even assured me that he'd kicked the girlfriend out for the occasion.

What a crazy group. And all awesome. He seemed to attract similarly spirited humans, even if he was pretending to be an average guy. Karl tried to get me to share his bed, but I refused. When I returned from the bathroom, I found that he had stolen mine. I slept on the floor. There was no way I was taking their bed!

I had hoped to leave the following day, but I didn't yet have a bicycle and I was too hungover. I tried my best to make magic happen, but that came in the form of chilling in the park with Karl and his friends. When the girlfriend arrived, I stopped breathing and eventually escaped to find Johan for a coffee and water. I couldn't bear the sight of alcohol. I returned to Karl's and knocked quietly to be let in. When I realised that it was the wrong door, I contemplated just sleeping in the hallway. I didn't want to be inside anyway, but I knew I deserved better and that wasn't the answer.

I eventually made it in and, for the first time in more than a month, I slept in the same bed twice.

I woke up to a homemade breakfast, the girlfriend had fried up a feast. It tasted as deliciously guilty as I felt. I desperately scanned the internet for bicycles, there had to be something, I needed to leave. No luck. I prayed someone would respond to the bikes I'd inquired about the previous days. I took a deep breath and tried to buy time by visiting Forex and picking up some kanelbullar[15] because I couldn't leave without having one with Karl.

I decided to leave anyway. I tied a sign to my backpack and hoped for the best. "Vill du salja din cykel?[16] I need a bike, otherwise, I'm walking to Amsterdam." I wasn't even joking.

"How do you feel about the chill?" Karl had asked as he walked me down the street on a cardboard run.

"You mean about leaving?"

"No, the other chill," he replied with his Karlish eyes piercing mine.

"Mate, I'm messed up. I have to go."

He didn't reply. And I was too scared to ask how he was.

We hugged each other. Again.

"See you again, maybe?" I said as emotionlessly as I could.

"You will," he said, pulling me in for another embrace.

I broke myself free, I didn't want to cycle, I didn't want to leave his arms, I didn't want to leave him. But right then, I had to get as far away as I possibly could so I could simply breathe. I needed air.

---

[15] Cinnamon buns.

[16] Do you want to sell me your bicycle?

10

Dyspnoeic

I *almost ran,* but I was carrying a lot of things, so it was more of an awkward stumble. A few blocks later somebody pointed me to a place where a caring stranger assured me I may find exactly what I was looking for: I-reCycle. I walked two levels underground and found the place a little eerie. Then again, I was dazed and overwhelmed and still not breathing.

"Can we help?"

They didn't laugh when I told them I needed a bike to cycle to the Netherlands on. And they didn't seem surprised that I was leaving the same day. While there were many beautiful bikes, the trusty employees managed to talk me out of more bad life decisions. After some digging, we found a sturdy steel-framed beauty which they fitted out with a luggage rack and some panniers while they entertained me with their terrible jokes. Trying to pile everything onto the bike was impossible, so I did an emergency "Summer clean" and disposed of some of my favourite dresses. I was in a season of parting with all sorts of my favourite things and I was emotionally disconnected from everything.

I still stalled in leaving. I always stall when changing life chapters, the numbed emotions don't numb the fear. I wanted to give up already, but I suddenly remembered that I was on an adventure with God and then the journey began.

I struggled to ride up the "hill" from the second-story basement. And then I proceeded to get lost in the city and cycled back past Karl's apartment twice. Circles and wrong turns all through Stockholm before I asked some cyclists for help. The university history lecturer told me to follow them. His wife led us on a beautiful detour through the forest and her brother Morty showed me to the perfect camping ground for the night.

I can't call it a perfect night's sleep with all the light and animals and guilt. But I did get to stretch my body out. And it was a great spot to savour my morning coffee in before feeling the flight reflux surfacing inside. The easiest way to deal with heartache is to run away from it.

I didn't pay much attention to where I was going and I cycled as hard and as fast as I could. I didn't care so much where I was going, as long as Stockholm was getting further and further away from me. In the greater scheme of things, I was headed for the Netherlands, but right then all I could think about was getting out of Sweden. I needed to distance myself from my stuff, from the crazy happenings, and from Karl.

It was an adventure. And a crazy one at that. On-lookers must have thought I was deranged with all the fervency I had burning inside me. I couldn't stop though, because I still couldn't breathe and I needed air. Pretty boats… I didn't stop. Beautiful landscapes, I didn't stop. My butt hurt; I didn't stop. Flat tyre, I had no option.

I tried to ask for help, but everyone ignored me. I asked in a restaurant, but they couldn't be bothered. I was unprepared. I was invisible. My off-line maps suggested there was a fuel station only two kilometres away. I put my backpack on my back and started walking, carrying my bike in one arm and the bear in the other. Yup, I was definitely invisible. I was struggling, I was on the verge of tears, and my giant fluffy companion was not much better, he kept getting his limbs in the way. I hated Sweden. I hated Swedes. I…

"Are you okay?"

What! Was somebody actually talking to me?

"Are you okay?"

I looked up to see a friendly smile and suddenly the world was okay again.

"It's just a flat tyre," I replied.

He took my bag and helped carry my bike while he pushed his.

"I think I have a repair kit," he said as we made our way toward the fuel station.

"Actually, this is silly, let me just go get my car."

I made myself comfortable and sat down on my backpack to write, not caring that I looked like the real gyspsies that seemed to be loitering all over Sweden. It was finally time to write, to try and put pen to paper and connect with my emotions. Who am I kidding? I filled three pages with doodles. But he was true to his word and returned with a repair kit and a bike rack.

"Mori," he said after I had introduced myself.

We fixed my flat and he added a casual, "There is a trans party in town tonight if you want to join?"

Mori felt like my only friend in the world. The vodka we consumed at the BBQ before we went out was not.

I danced away my worries in the nightly daylight. Something inside me felt alive again. And as I curled up on the sleeper couch, I thanked God for the flat tyre.

Many other flat tyres lined the road to Norway, but none were as memorable. When my outer wheel tore and I had the inner tube bulging out, God somehow kept it intact for the five and a half Swedish miles[17] until I reached the next bicycle shop. My inner turmoil was still a raging storm, but the forests and fields and lakes and rivers of Sweden gave me hope and every night I baptized myself in some sort of water. Every day I was shaped into a new person, tackling each challenge as it came, but still not daring to breathe. People remained distant, but every now and then, a

---

[17] +/-57 kilometres (for Swedish miles are not like regular miles).

caring stranger would surprise me with a hug or some fruit, or even just a smile. They meant even more seeing as I wasn't expecting them.

On my final morning in Sweden, it poured with rain and I was hesitant to begin. I lay doodling in my tent until the water levels had risen so much that it threatened to pour into my tent through the mosquito mesh. The ground was saturated and it was time to move. When the rain calmed to a drizzle, I rolled up my tent and threw everything onto the bike, securing it with a poncho. (It's never convenient travelling with a laptop and even less with a giant teddy bear that weighs 2 kg when it's dry). What was I doing with my life?

"Trust me," reminded God.

The cycle path veered through a forest. There was no protection and the rains were bucketing down. I started to climb the muddy tracks as the streams flooded down towards me. I was pedalling upstream. I sang at the top of my lungs as I pushed. The last push, the final cleansing. And finally, in the not-so-serene shelter of a bus stop, I opened up my mouth to breathe in the fresh air of Norway.

For the first time, possibly ever, I booked myself into a hotel. I deserved it, and I wanted to be dry. I wanted to shower off the past. I wanted.

The night was dry, warm and beautiful. And so were my belongings, the receptionist helped me clean them all. She also made sure the Polish guests shared their beer with me and invited me for breakfast. Refreshed, I cycled off to explore the beautiful country.

Crossing the border back to Sweden didn't bother me in the slightest, I felt new. Either the country had completely changed, or I had. People wanted to help me and wanted to get to know me. I was no longer invisible. (Also, some of the houses were not red.)

After the third time, some girls passed me in their car, they stopped me in my tracks. And then forced me to go and drink fika[18] with them. The love and peace and twerking that the night held as we jammed and danced assured me that I was a new person. Their hugs and their words reminded me that I was not the worst person in the world. And hearing their stories made me step into my own. I was once again reminded that I

---

[18] Swedish coffee.

was on an adventure with God[19].

Every night I found a perfect place to camp. I sometimes spent a whole day cycling in the rain and somehow still managed to find a dry place to sleep at night. The days were so long that it didn't matter what time I started or when I pitched my tent, it was simply taking each day as it came and listening to the inner voice that kept me on a schedule for meeting legends and seeing beautiful creatures. My life was a movie script by a universe-class director.

I met only two other cycle tourers before I met Oliver. He passed me twice before he dared to talk to me. I had so much junk on my bike that he wanted to make certain that I wasn't one of "those can ladies." In all fairness, the way I had strapped everything onto my bike, I looked like one.

"If only we could have a beer together," he said.

I beamed, earlier that day, I had passed the Systembolaget[20] and actually found it open. For the first time on my cycle, I was carrying two beers. I offered him one and we sat down on a grassy knoll to savour its deliciousness. It didn't even matter that they were warm. We needed to hear each other's stories.

We were headed in opposite directions, so we cycled into a quiet suburb and pitched our tents on the slug-infested lawn. We wondered how long it would take for our posh neighbours to come and complain. They didn't. But the following morning, the neighbourhood came out to meet us and greet us. They were proud that their little suburb could feel like home to such adventurous souls.

I left Sweden full of life and my blood pulsed even stronger through Denmark as I caught up with a fellow traveller that I'd met in the Philippines years earlier. The weather was so bad and her vibe was so good that my one-night stay in Copenhagen stretched to five awesome days with Mia. Denmark apartments have shoots you can slide your garbage down.

---

[19] I also need to mention that I'd had another awesome offer to stay with someone kind and friendly that same day. But the voice inside me told me to say no. I couldn't work it out at the time, but sometimes we have to turn down good things so that we can get better ones.

[20] The bottle store and the only place allowed to sell alcohol above 3.5% in Sweden.

And when it comes to booking your laundry, you don't use a whiteboard or paper, you lock it in with an actual lock. In Denmark, there are trees full of children's dummies[21] where they hang them when they are ready to leave childhood behind. I was tempted to pick one up.

It was sad saying goodbye, but the world keeps getting smaller and there would be a next time. Mia had been a great tour guide, friend and coach. She taught me how the phenomenal cycle paths worked. They were so easy to simply follow without having to consult maps, an art I have never been particularly good at. Life was great, but it was raining again, so I decided to find a bridge to camp under. I got chased away by an angry swan. The next bridge was full of intimidating fishermen. Darkness came and I was still searching. I didn't have any lights because I hadn't needed any yet. Eventually I [literally] crashed into some woods and the ground under the canopy of trees felt relatively dry so I simply slept there. I awoke to the galloping of hooves hustling in my direction, at the last minute they swerved and carried on to wherever they were racing. I love my guardian angels.

Germany flew by very quickly. I was not pedalling to run anymore, I was pedalling to breathe because I felt more alive than ever. A woman started screaming something at me so I stopped to apologise because I had no idea what I was doing wrong.

"Oh, you're English," said the ferocious woman with a smile.

"I was just asking why you are cycling here when there is a beautiful cycle path down there by the water?"

I made the same mistake a few days later when I was pitching my tent in a field so I could stay dry from the encroaching storm.

"I'm sorry," I said to the angry Germans, "I just want to stay dry."

They were simply inviting me to stay at their house for exactly that reason. I don't know who else needs to know this, but Germans are not as fierce as they sound.

It was a Sunday, so the ferry I had planned to take to the Netherlands was

---

[21] Some countries would call them 'pacifiers.

not running. I had delayed changing countries earlier because I wanted to make sure that I was ready for it. My dad was Dutch and a lot of my family whom I had never met still lived there. I'd had the passport for years, it was half of who I was, and I wanted to make sure that I was fully me on arrival.

I'd battled the headwind all of the North Sea and now I was battling it again through fields of sheep and swarms of flying ducks as it tried to keep me from arrival. The rain came too but it made me push even harder. It was a battle scene to make my triumphant arrival across the border to my fatherland.

UNEMPLOYMENT LOOKS BETTER WITH A TAN

11

Heineken, Cheese & other Absurdities

I ***hugged every person I could find at the border,*** telling them how I'd finally reached my fatherland. It had been weeks since my last shower so those hugs were memorable. They carefully deliberated my inquiry regarding the best route to get to Groningen.

The rain plummeted down and, at first, I tried to hide from it. But I gave up eventually and went pedalling all-out, full-blown until my phone died. I knew exactly where I was heading, but I had no idea how to navigate there. I was forced to stop for a beer.

Joy was outside waiting for me. She had the South African flag and balloons lining the doorway and an African-themed room ready for me. She'd known me since before I was born and had been the maid of honour at my parents' wedding. It was good to be in family company and I was spoilt to have an enthusiastic guide to show me around my heritage land.

I'd agreed to house-sit for her and was excited to spend two weeks in the same place. I knew about the dogs, but she didn't tell me that she was also looking after somebody's cockatoo, her stepdad, and another adopted elderly lady whose own family didn't care for her. Joy was a saint. She was also in her 70s, but I could not keep up.

A week after she left me, I fell into depression. It dawned on me that I had virtually nothing in the world, not even a plan. Only a dirty teddy bear and some scars that previous adventures had decorated me with. I hid. I avoided people. I didn't want anyone to see me for the fraud that I was.

On the cycle out to meet my family in Assen for the first time, I had a mild meltdown and a panic attack. They accepted me anyway. Exactly as I was. They were of a legendary nature. My dad's cousin, who shared his name, was the perfect person to teach me all about our family history and tell me a bit more about who we were. We'd been sailors and travellers and awesome. My dad had died when I was very young and my grandparents not long afterwards, so there were plenty of questions about this side of the family. Herman drove me and my bicycle home and I hugged him goodbye feeling somewhat restored and very grateful.

Life was full of responsibilities and chores, but there was something else plaguing me, too. When was the last time I had my period? Stockholm. I'd bled all over everything. It had been the heaviest period of my life, in every sense of the phrase. And that had been several weeks earlier. It took me a few days to do it, but I cycled over to the closest city and went into the pharmacy to get a test. I couldn't do it in the village because someone might see me and word would get back to Joy which would in turn get back to my mom and... Okay, so how do I do this?

It took a whole morning to prepare myself for the test. I wanted to think about what either result would mean. If I were pregnant, how would I feel about it, what would I do? In fact, the likelihood of pregnancy was not small, that had been some baby-making sex in the smultronstället. I peed in the jar, dripped it on the stick and went on with menial house chores to try and distract myself. Did I want Karl's baby?

I dumped the test in a paper bag inside a cereal bag inside another bag six blocks away and went for a long walk to clear my head. It rained. I didn't care.

Joy was coming back soon so I began to panic. I needed life plans. She would want me to be around for ages, out of guilt or duty, or maybe even out of pleasure. But I didn't want that. I couldn't take that. I desperately started job hunting and plan forming. I also did another pregnancy test, just to make sure. I may have made premature plans out of desperation, but I felt kind of good about them.

It was good to have her back, but I felt like I was in her space. I've always worried about being in the way or being a burden. Too often I have left beautiful spaces too soon. Before people could see the true me, just in case I was not good enough. And unfortunately, before I could experience the true them as well. It's quite something to realize that everyone is human and nobody is perfect. What a gift it is to show our true selves and accept others for exactly who they are, too. I'm learning to relax and simply enjoy the company of those around me, but guilt is something that has tormented generations of my family!

The day after her return, her elderly adoptee died. I'm glad all the pets were still in good shape and I am glad that Tante Anna had not been left in my personal care, I was just requested to visit her and she wasn't a particularly nice person to visit. This showed; I was one of only four people who attended her funeral. Staying with Joy, I didn't exactly have a choice in the matter. The open casket did her no justice. That was Wednesday.

By Thursday I was sitting at the tiny airport ready to fly out straight back to where I had come from, straight back to Stockholm.

UNEMPLOYMENT LOOKS BETTER WITH A TAN

12

Trouble Brews

I did not tell Karl I was coming. But that didn't matter, I probably wouldn't see him anyway. Still, my eyes were on the lookout as I boarded a bus from the airport to the city centre. I passed so many landmarks I had raced past on my escape. I passed Karl's apartment. My heart was a tribal drum, at a human sacrifice as I tried to ease into my seat and remember that God was in control. I was still on an adventure with Him.

Marcus and his sister were waiting for me. They were all smiles and full of energy despite the lateness of the hour. They shared the same blood, but she had managed to secure a normal life of kids, marriage and routine. He on the other hand had fled Sweden by boat at the age of 15, put himself through high school, sailed the world, joined the military, and never quite managed to settle. He was an interesting character, but not quite what I had been expecting.

S/Y *Havsfrun*, my new temporary home, had been his for five years. He had a house too, but she was his home. It was time to take her to warmer waters where she could be sailed for longer than the three months in the year that Sweden warranted. It was time to take her to the Mediterranean, and I was there to help with the mission. I hoped that I wouldn't disappoint.

She was a 43-foot Moody ketch, from 1977, but in immaculate condition, with mostly original parts. He was a 46-year-old soft-hearted Swede. His military years made him meticulous and perfection-driven, but I could still see the human within. He sat down with a glass of wine and sentenced me to the shower. I assured him that I'd had one only a few hours earlier, but he was a clean freak. The sun rose. Things were strange.

The weather forecast was not great, so we delayed departure another day. And while I enjoyed the boat, I more enjoyed exploring the natural surroundings and talking to strangers. After hibernating in the Netherlands, I had almost forgotten the art of befriending randoms. Somehow, I now needed to again.

We had a later departure than planned, but it was perfectly timed in the golden hours of duskly glow. The winds had calmed and the rains had finally stopped. *Havsfrun* was immaculately over-clean. We still had the wind kissing us on the nose, but it carried with it the scent of the ocean, the smell of [my] home. We anchored near a liten ö[22] for the night and I allowed myself to have a small glass of wine. But should I be drinking? I tried to put my fears aside and enjoy dinner, but my mind was still a troubled ocean.

I sat soaking up the sun as boats Sunday-ed past and a spider sat busily spinning a web. I tried to chill out and relax, but I had too much guilt bearing down on my shoulders. There were so many people I should be seeing, so many jobs I should be doing. There was so much that ... Guilt is a funny thing. Whoever invented it is probably quite a rich and powerful man or a Jezebel of a woman. Some people seem to effortlessly shake it while others let it pile up until they are crippled by it. Marcus ran circles around his own life and wouldn't let me do a thing. It made me feel even more guilty, why was I there? I needed to earn my keep. I needed to give more than I received. I needed to shake the guilt.

---

[22] Small island.

At one a.m. I took a seasick pill to help me sleep. It worked perfectly. So much so that I overslept my watch time and left Marcus doing a very long shift. I wanted to go outside and enjoy the sunshine, but the strict rules about changing clothing every time I entered or left the cockpit made me too lazy to do it. "You can't go bringing salt inside, now, can you?" (Oh, the horrors!) Instead, I tried to piece the world together through the portholes. There was no comfortable place to perch. There was also no coffee, it was "too dangerous"[23] and it was a waste of propane". I was not allowed to cook either, because I might use too much propane. I was not allowed to touch any of the dials. I was not allowed to alter course. I was simply to stand watch and awaken the captain if anything needed to be done.

In my current mental phase, it made sense. I believed that I was unable to do anything useful, I felt unworthy of sitting, and I felt dirty. So, I accepted my hover in the airless cabin taking in segmented views of the paradise that surrounded me. I gave Marcus the right to believe I was worthless. My uselessness increased in leaps and bounds as every day the list of things I could not do grew longer.

We left the Swedish waters and avoided colliding with all the Danish wind farms. We were nearing Germany, and it was the middle of the night when the boat started spinning around out of control.

"Marcus," I yelled. And then again louder, "Marcus!!!"

Fearing another lecture, I assured him I hadn't touched a thing. By the time it happened for the third time, we deduced that it must be all the shrunken shrapnel from the war, setting our compasses and autopilot out of sync. Marcus took over my watch and I didn't feel like being useless, so I went to bed. In the early hours of the morning, I lay awake and wondered what kind of day we were in for. I wondered if, by some miracle, we would be allowed coffee.

---

[23] In all fairness, hot liquids are rather dangerous on a moving vessel (I know this first hand). But so is leaving the house, crossing the road, and battling bureaucracy… and we do these things anyway! What is the point of being alive if you can't ~~enjoy it~~ drink coffee?

The Kiel Canal was longer and busier than the Panama Canal but, without the bureaucracy, it was so much easier. Boats of all shapes and sizes filled the lock and the water lowered and spat us out on the other side. We dodged all sorts of monstrous vessels heading in the opposite direction and docked in Rensburg to shelter from the incessant headwind.

I may have skipped out on my crewing responsibility because I saw a beautiful wooden schooner with a British flag and I could not resist the opportunity to maybe acquire a few English books. I had a tour of the vessel and delayed further with a drink with the crew. I returned to an angry captain who was slaving away heating a tin of meat for dinner. But I now had both books and chocolate in hand, making it all worthwhile.

I could not bear the scent of the "food", so I skipped dinner and went for a walk through the town to clear my head. I knew Marcus wanted company, but I was starting to pay more attention to my own needs first. I breathed in the crisp evening air and followed my lack of direction to get myself lost in the little town. And as I took the first step to care for myself, my body started to fall back into sync. My period started, at last. I bought beer to celebrate it and enjoyed the beverage without guilt. Still, my head was not quite where it should have been. Why was I there? There were so many more enjoyable things I could be doing instead of subjecting myself to military consignment. I didn't have a choice now, I was committed. I was already aboard, and this was my penance to pay.

We began again at dawn and continued our transit through the Kiel Canal, into the Elbe. We were spat into the North Sea to round the Netherlands. The North Sea was glass. Marcus had sailed it dozens of times and had never seen it so calm. Our engine worked overtime. My body ached. I wasn't sure if it was stress leaving my body from the confirmation that I was not pregnant or perhaps Lyme disease from all the tick bites. Or perhaps something else? Four a.m. was not the best time to be wondering about these things alone at the helm with the soundtrack of snoring roaring through the air. And definitely not while I was crossing busy shipping canals.

The sun rose as we passed Rotterdam and the day transformed into a Bluebird. My dad would have been 65 that day. I wondered what he thought about me drifting about the planet the way I did. It was almost as if he was smiling upon me, keeping all the busiest shipping lanes clear and keeping us safe as we began crossing the English Channel. I raised a glass of wine to him that night, but only one, people were swimming across the channel and I wanted to be extra vigilant.

The sunrise was fire and the day was even more sunny than the previous one had been. We had Irish coffee for breakfast as we dodged fishing vessels off the British coast. The day was wonderful. And then it got weird.

"Adeena, should I warm you some water for a shower?"

I was used to the skipper urging me to over-pursue personal hygiene, but this seemed different. And no, I did not want to wash in the cockpit in the cold setting sun. And yes, I could wash myself thank you very much.

"Another glass of wine?"

I was tempted, but I decided that it was better to keep my wits and drink water instead. The captain poured himself another glass of whiskey while I ate dinner. I took the opportunity for an early night. Probably the earliest night ever. There were weird vibes. Was it just the alcohol?

I couldn't think about anything other than jumping ship. These were the thoughts that kept me awake that night and I was still thinking about them that morning, the 29th of August, as I had forced the captain to go to bed. What a relief! I had been more than a little uncomfortable as he had cornered me in a way that I could not sink any deeper into the wall to escape him. He was drunk, he felt sexy. But he had now risen to new levels of disgust that I just was not willing to put up with. Had he really finished off two bottles of whisky?

At least we were sailing again so I didn't have to hear the engine roar, although that may have drowned out some of the snoring. There still wasn't much wind, but we no longer had motoring as an option as we were almost completely out of fuel. The fishing vessels that tried to run us over were rather concerning, but I had all my wits in check and I was taking no chances with anything.

The captain arose to take over, as he always did, so I went back to bed. Again I tossed and turned restlessly. I heard him call my name. Was it my watch already?

"Adeena"

I ignored it after I checked the time.

"Adeena," he called more ardently.

I reluctantly opened the door to my drunken skipper.

"I have decided that we will skip Falmouth and sail straight for Spain."

I rubbed my eyes and made sure that I was awake. In any other setting, I would have imagined this as a joke. We had almost no fuel, and very little food aboard and that man loved consuming both.

"The winds are great so we will actually sail," he said, "I thought you would be overjoyed at the suggestion."

As much as I had wished for more sailing, this was not the way to do it.

I did what anyone would do in my situation, I excused myself to the bathroom. Now, you have probably seen it in movies, but I had no idea, until that day, that people really did it. I pep-talked myself in the mirror. I returned with feigned braveness and told him that I felt like I was not needed aboard as I was not allowed to do anything. I told him straight that he had made me feel uncomfortable the day before and had come on far too strong. I reminded him that we had both agreed on no relationships or anything of the sort before I had joined the ship and that I still held to that agreement. He stared at me stunned. I was just going to leave it at that and let it slide, but the words came from nowhere: "This is a big boat that you have transformed into a life raft."

He told me that I should go back to bed for a couple of hours so that he could think.

Of course, I couldn't sleep. I lay in bed with my phone in hand using the GPS to check which course he was steering. When I could lay still no more and I heard the motor purring, I stepped outside.

"Everything okay?"

He went straight to the cockpit, so I stayed in. I guess he had decided on Falmouth anyway, he wouldn't be burning the last of our fuel otherwise. Unless… my mind raced, was he trying to get us forced to be stuck at sea together?

13

The Rule of Thumb

We *moored instead of docking.* He was too afraid that they might smell the alcohol seeping through him. No kidding, he reeked! I may have avoided seasickness, but the mere thought of making out with him made me gag. He swigged whisky straight from the bottle as he spoke on the phone.

"Looks like I got myself, new crew," he said as he finished the last dregs of what was a reasonably full bottle not much earlier.

"So, will it be the three of us to Spain? Or am I dumping you here?"

"I think you already know the answer to that question," I replied, pouring myself a glass of wine.

He opened up another bottle and, realising that there had been no cooking and still not being permitted to use the stove, I helped myself to a bowl of muesli while I finished my wine.

UNEMPLOYMENT LOOKS BETTER WITH A TAN

All packed and breakfasted, I sat in the cockpit. A very hungover man started the engine and puttered *Havsfrun* to the dock. It was a nice farewell and it felt right. He did pause to tell me that he loved me, that he couldn't help himself. I knew that he had a good heart, but the military had wrecked him and he had yet to reclaim his life. I hugged him, told him to be kind to himself, and I never looked back. It was a new season of life where I let go of things and kept moving forward. And that day I had a long route ahead of me, my destination was 144 miles away. I paused at the first garbage bins to collect some cardboard and then ran up the road as the rains plummeted down.

I held out my sign and the first car stopped. I did the limbo to squeeze in under all the building supplies and a ladder. The smiling construction worker introduced me to his kids and told them all about the power of thumb and alternative means of transport. I'm not sure I would be their mother's favourite person, but I hoped that she would approve. The next ride was a fancy BMW that I never suspected would stop, the nicer cars never do. The kind driver left me with hugs and good energy.

Phil Philips was a fascinating Welshman with very strong opinions about Brexit and a very interesting-sounding wife. The depression made her eat. The eating made her fat. The fat made her never leave the house, except occasionally to shop. And when she shopped, she bought three of every item. Two of them in sizes she would never fit again. One spare bedroom was for one size and the other for the other. All were neatly wrapped in plastic to keep them fresh. It poured as I said my goodbyes in Bristol.

I waited for ages until John and his 17-month-old son pulled up. They were heading for Liverpool. I had a strange feeling at first, but he was undeniably cool. His wife had walked out on him four months earlier leaving him to care for the two youngest while running three companies. I was struck with respect for him and completely shocked when he went out of his way to drop me off in Stratford-upon-Avon.

"Did you know that Shakespeare was born here?" I asked as we passed a sign telling me just that.

He just kept smiling and dropped me on the doorstep of my destination.

Sharna wasn't home yet, so I made myself at home and wondered if she was as cool as I imagined, or if this would be awkward. I didn't have long to ponder as the legend herself came bursting through the door in running gear. My soul started renewing itself while basking in her awesomeness! I went to bed buzzing; I was too excited about life to sleep.

I was out partying when someone yelled at me because I had neglected my kid.

"What kid?" I asked.

"Your baby."

I hadn't even been certain that I was pregnant. And what? Five months premature! That kid was tiny. I thought I was dreaming when I was handed the kid. MY KID! What the flip?!

"You need to breastfeed," said a stranger.

I looked down at my boobs, yes, they seemed a little bit bigger, but would it work? Would you believe that milk came out and the kid started sucking? I say "the kid" because I was such a bad parent that I couldn't even tell if it was male or female. I put the tiny baby down, chatted to someone, got distracted, and lost it.

"We are leaving now," said someone.

I was about to leave when I suddenly remembered that I had a kid and started searching frantically for it. It was gone. Why was it so tiny? Ages later, somebody told me to forget about it, that I wasn't ready to be a mum.

"But, but, but...."

I wanted to cry out that I could change, I could do this, but... I searched harder. They were right of course, but still, I didn't give up. Hours later I finally found the kid when I sat down on the couch to cry. That's when the kid started crying too, I was sitting on it. Like a cell phone, it had been lost in the stuffing of the couch.

Sharna had already left for work, so I went for a long run to try and combat the weird dream. It was a dreamy county too, very Shakespearian and beautiful in the Autumn sun. Sharna returned before I had even finished writing postcards. She's the only person that I know who will buy two whole loaves of bread just to make ducks happy. She is also the only person that I know who refuses to cook the same meal twice. And she is creative enough that she will probably never have to.

I'd met her in passing in Papua New Guinea the year before and felt like I needed to get to know her. I was right! A couple of days with her had my soul restored and my body recaffeinated. It was nice to share and talk about life, adventure, men, and everything in between. She got it. And I got all her condoms because she had found "the one" and didn't need them anymore.

Sharna was running the Swindon marathon that Sunday. She had never before been to Swindon. Oddly enough, it just so happened that she needed to drive there on the day I'd agreed to meet Emily.

Em was new to Swindon too, a proud resident, and still as much of a legend as ever. The only difference was that she had changed her career from Outdoor Instructor to Landscape Designer and had changed continents at the same time. I had met her hitchhiking. It was thanks to her that I got my instructing job in Australia. And thanks to her I got my visa to do a second year too. We had farmed chickens together, drank almost every form of alcohol that there was, and fortunately never killed any of the kids we had in our care. It had been six years since we had last seen each other, but it felt like no time had passed at all.

The next day she was back to work and I was back on the road. I had a series of interesting hitched rides before I got picked up by a "Professional Nutter". I thought he was joking, but he assured me that the crazier he got, the more money the government paid him. He used to be a school teacher, but at some point, he simply forgot which class he was teaching. His car was a disaster zone, but his smile assured me that there was goodness in him. When his teaching was reported, he was taken for psychiatric testing and put through a series of electric shock therapies. When that didn't work, they turned to pills. At some point, he started a family, but that fell apart too, probably because he had stopped taking the pills. I wondered if I was actually okay sitting in his car. With every sentence he spoke, he turned the radio up a little more. He smiled, I had stopped smiling.

"Don't you want kids?" he asked.

"I first have to find the right man," I replied.

"Well, if you're into septuagenarians, then I'm your man."

He turned the radio up again and told me how some or other famous person, who was four years older than him, had just given birth to twins. And then he asked me to marry him. I declined, but he didn't seem to be too shaken up about my refusal. He dropped me at the Wetherspoons in Brighton and I took his advice and enjoyed it.

Two rides later, I was back on the ferry to France. This time I even paid for the ticket and mingled with the other foot passengers. Both of them. The ferry ride was short and sweet and while I did try and sleep, I needn't have bothered.

I drank coffee and munched on fresh morning croissants while I waited for the sun to rise. Then it was all systems go and a ride in a truck and, a couple of cars later, I was dropped at a beach in Normandy. I didn't have time to prepare myself for the massive hug that ensued.

I wasn't expecting Damien's family to be so "normal," or welcoming. They had roasted a guinea fowl and made sweet potato gnocchi on a spread with cheese and wine for my arrival ceremony (or perhaps this was their typical lunch spread). Either way, I felt like I was the Queen. But maybe that was because I had come straight from the UK. We took an afternoon wander as he showed me all his favourite spots. The evening disappeared in an adventure through a series of bunkers and interesting forts. Damien will always be one of my favourite adventure buddies, there isn't a dull bone in his body. We cycled through the hills, hiked, explored, and ate. Man did we eat. I seemed to be having a culinary tour of Europe.

I made a rash decision to try and catch another friend in Paris before he flew out. So, I left Damien's land prematurely and hit the road again. I was still buzzing with life. Still excited. And I was carefree, not even so much as worrying when the police shouted at me for being on the highway.

I rode in my first electric car. When I stuck my thumb out again, a truck stopped. I peered through the window. One of the men shot mild pangs of terror through my being, but the other had such kind eyes that I couldn't say no. We tried conversation but gave up and turned the truck into a disco instead, all the way through to the outskirts of Paris. I should have hopped out there, I could see the Eiffel Tower and it was still light. But they assured me they would drop off the truck and motorbike me straight through to the centre.

"Ten minutes!"

But ten minutes later we were even further away and they had picked up someone else. I was moved to the cargo hold. I began to wonder if they were in fact kidnapping me. I had taken selfies with them to send to my mom and one of them had already added me on Facebook, so if they were, they were doing a pretty bad job of it. Still, I was unsettled and I made sure to send friends their pictures and the Facebook link, just in case. I was enormously grateful that I had finally invested in a European SIM card and was connected. I carefully followed our route with my phone's GPS.

We dropped off the truck and there was a motorbike waiting, as promised. Perhaps the worry was all in my head? I wasn't quite sure how to balance all of my belongings, but we made it work. My new friend made me hold on to him tight. I refused. He insisted. I have never been much good at riding bitch so it was a tough ride for both of us. He stopped in the most bizarre spot and signalled for five minutes. I refused. He insisted and pointed to what must have been his apartment. I shook my head and sat down on the pavement. He signalled that it was a dangerous neighbourhood. I stayed sitting. He pointed to a car. His car?

"Five minutes!"

It was a losing battle, I followed him in.

"Five minutes!"

He locked the door, battered the windows and closed all the curtains. I was afraid. I used the toilet to send Rohan a message and a location, but I still hoped for the best. When I returned, he was on the phone making a serious conversation. I pointed to the time and told him I needed to go. Why could he not understand that my friend was only in town for one night and I wanted to see him? I was in a hurry. He hung up and lay down. I yelled at him. He told me to come and lie next to him. I yelled some more. He sat up and signalled that his back was hurting, could I give him a massage? I walked to the door and tried to unlock it, where was the key? He stood up pleading for me to calm down. I called Rohan. Did anyone with him speak French?

"I'll call back in a minute."

My new friend was now on the couch and back on the phone. Who was he speaking to? I was now almost certain that he was trying to ship me off somewhere, even if I wasn't blonde or particularly exotic. He motioned for me to join him on the couch. I walked circles around the apartment looking for the keys yelling at him that I needed to go. Rohan called back. I now stopped pretending that everything was okay and filled him in that I thought that I was being kidnapped. His French-speaking friend did wonders in yelling at my captor. He looked at me apologetically and while he was on the phone distracted, I managed to sneak the keys from his pocket. He must have thought that I was finally trying to get friendly with him because he lay down on the couch and made room for me to join. He was calm. He took the conversation in stride and passed me back my phone.

"He just needs five minutes," said my translator.

I laughed and filled her in. I also told them that I was about to make a run for it and if they didn't hear from me in the next few minutes, they should please call the police. What a way to wreck Rohan's last night in Europe.

I picked up my stuff and ran for the door, unlocked it, and ventured out screaming to arouse the curiosity of all the neighbours who came out in support. The man was embarrassed and sheepish, but I didn't care. I ran down the road while he jumped on his bike and chased me. I eventually made it to the nearest tram station and breathed out.

It was only three minutes till the end of happy hour (23:57) when I hugged Rohan. I'd been only five km away from him at 19:02. I wanted to cry in relief, but decided to shove away emotions and simply bask in good company instead.

Rohan was a significant player in my life. When I had tried to find someone to hitchhike with in Vietnam, he had tracked me down and convinced me to cycle across Southeast Asia with him instead. Rohan had changed my life! And it was great to reunite, even just for a night.

His friend (my translator) led us back to her tiny cupboard-sized apartment and we carried on chilling through till the early morning when, after croissants and coffee, he hugged us both goodbye and flew back to Australia. Instead of a backpack, he carried a wheely trolley case. He was the same calibre of awesome, but some things had clearly changed!

I hung out in Paris for the morning and then decided to escape. I was back in the habit of running away from problems and emotions. I stopped on the side of the Rhine to gather my thoughts and eat a pan au chocolat. It hurt to think and I simply kept moving, even if I wasn't sure where I was going. I thought of heading back to Damien, but that was counter-productive; moving backwards. So, I stuck out my thumb and started towards Germany. My phone beeped on the way and my destination was set. My first driver, Dick, was a photographer and exceptionally good at it. He dropped me at a fuel station and showered me in hugs and French kisses before helping me find a ride onward. The thing about being on an adventure with God is that he always knows what you need and when. And He is very good at giving us just that!

A truck and another car later, I was going to hop off in Nancy, but it was too late to be early and too early to be late. I agreed to stay in the vehicle until Strasbourg. When the tunnel was closed, I ended up spending the night in the passenger seat with the heater blaring. The driver was right, it was far too cold to camp in those mountains! Also, he was a good man with an endless supply of coffee. I was in great company.

The other side of the tunnel held strange people and situations that I shall speed over, for while I profess that hitchhiking is an awesome way to travel, there were an awful lot of people wanting more than just company that day. My psychology studies came in most useful as I tried to make the world a better place by reminding men that there was more to life than getting their dicks wet. I think that it was also to my advantage that I was transporting smelly French cheese as gifts.

I was only 30 km away from my destination when I met other hitchhikers. A father and son. They assured me that they didn't mind me sharing their spot, but they didn't have a sign and I knew I would be stealing their ride. I gave them mine and decided to give public transport a shot. I was trying to work out how to use the ticket machine when a group of gaggling American NGO workers invited me to use their group voucher, they had a free spot. And when I wanted to bus the last little leg, the driver waved me aboard for free.

It had been eight years since I had last seen Marc. He was both taller and more intelligent than I had remembered. We shared some beer and feasted on cheese as we caught up on adventures long past. Marc had been travelling for decades and had done his fair share of tour guiding. While most people I know aren't too fond of Stuttgart, his passion for it made it come alive. Marc worked at a school that was closed for the summer, so I got to use the sick room as my bedroom. It was a good place to diagnose my thoughts and it was a great place to start admitting truths and combating the lies that I had allowed myself to believe. The mind is a powerful thing. It needs at least as much tending to as the body.

I had more hugs to distribute so, a few days later, I hit the road again and turned South. I took shelter in Tuborg from the storm that hit. Well-caffeinated, I continued to Rotenberg. Mika had just finished work when I arrived and the timing was perfect. She hadn't changed one bit, only her plans and her inner strength.

The more people I reunited with, the more my soul grew. There were so many stories that I needed to hear. And so many people that I needed to encourage. So many people that grew and developed me. Mika's life may have felt like it was a mess, but the mess made her stronger and turned her into a fighter. She was stronger than ever!

I remember those talks we'd had late at night, on Schooner Havsström, she had come such a long way since then. Despite the hardships she currently faced, I looked at how much joy she carried with her. That filled me with joy, too.

Mika dreamed of going back to her tribe in New Zealand where life was good and free and pure. But for now, she was stuck in a one-bedroom apartment in Rotenberg doing what her parents couldn't. A rainbow streaked the sky as the rain began to pour. The other park-dwellers fled, but the tree we had perched under kept us perfectly dry. We were exactly where we were meant to be. As had become the norm on my adventure, dinner was a feast of love. It was cooked with an assortment of Aldi groceries and spread in a room filled with the sunflowers that we had just picked. Sunflowers were also quickly becoming a part of my journey; I was leaving them with friends all along my path.

"Where are you going next?" asked Mika when I started packing up my things.

"I'm hitchhiking to Lichtenstein to get a beer."

And while I was close, it was a lot more of a challenging destination than I had anticipated. Switzerland was spectacular and I paused to savour a beer in the postcard surrounds. I walked a lot because cars were few and seemed to be blind to the gypsy strolling down the road. I finally crossed the border in the dark and ventured into the first pub I found. I cheered a stranger as I fulfilled the day's mission. It was too late to return, so I ventured off to find the only hostel. I would reevaluate my life plans in the morning.

The internet booking sites told me that it was full. It was also almost 11 p.m. when I finally arrived, so I doubted that there would be anyone to check me in.

"The door code is three three six nine," yelled a man having a cigarette on the steps.

And as soon as I entered, someone came running.

"You're not a group of 15," said the smiling man.

I confirmed this and, as if it was predestined, I took one of the beds set aside for them. Because they never arrived, I had a dorm all to myself. It was an expensive night's stay, but the friendly night watchman was not kidding, the breakfast more than made up for it. It was also the first accommodation I had paid for since Norway.

I walked back across the border into Switzerland, and then patiently waited for what felt like forever. Normally, it would not have bothered me, but this time I was getting stressed because I had places to be. I'd booked a bus ticket from Zurich and I only had a few hours to get there. An assortment of colourful people made the seemingly impossible possible, which was a big relief. I had two days to make it to London. I needed to cheat a little bit otherwise I would never make it in time.

A series of long and boring bus rides ensued. I broke up the trip in Paris where I met fellow adventurer Mylene for lunch. I'd last seen this beautiful legend when we had braved the fierce wonders of the land down under [Australia]. Fate had us venture the coastline by campervan. Together we foraged for food, learning to fish for survival and, when we failed, we learned how to digest whatever other creatures we could scavenge on the beach. She taught me how to play Patong. I taught her how to hitchhike. We enjoyed many laughs, beautiful beaches, and crazy epic adventures together. Six years later, she was still as awesome, beautiful, and crazy as ever! It was so worth dropping back in on Paris just to give her a hug!

The day's timings had all been perfect. I arrived in Paris at dawn and found vending machine coffee right next to a brilliantly skilled street musician who made me cry with the beautiful tunes that he poured straight off his soul and onto the keys of the community piano. I'd met good people everywhere I went and had excellent company for most of it. The next bus ride was much less painful because I was Zen and the seat next to me was vacant.

Back in London, I fought the temptation that MMMM Chicken seemed to offer and went to the off-license instead. I'm glad that Jarred got home when he did because the street was starting to get a bit sketchy. We crossed the road to his apartment and caught up on all the years that had passed. I may have been in a class with his sister, but in a school as small as ours, that didn't matter!

It was early morning when our eyes gave up before our mouths did. I had a busy day ahead of me. But I failed to find a birthday present and I failed to find a dress and I was late. It wasn't quite the "surprise party" Chloe had sold me over the phone, but Brendon was my baby brother and he does only turn 30 once. And it was well worth the trip just to have the honour of bestowing a surprise birthday hug upon him[24].

In the blink of an eye, I was back in the Netherlands. And the good people and happy reunions escalated so quickly that I was blown away by goodness and love. Luc, whom I had met in Saint Lucia years before, toured me through Ijburg and dropped me at a fuel station. I hitched back to my bicycle and Joy and Teddy. It wasn't the same travelling without Teddy. I had asked Marcus if I could bring him and his prompt response was, "I don't think that's a good idea."

I don't think any of it was a good idea, but I had some lessons I needed to learn and some extra hugs to glean.

I was still working on life plans but they seemed to be taking shape on their own. I left Joy's and set off to cycle around my Fatherland and

---

[24] As well as a planned one with his beautiful girlfriend, Chloe.

make the most of it before I had to escape. Winter was coming and my new plans were almost finalized.

14

Navigating the Nether Regions

I hadn't exactly enjoyed the Netherlands the first time I'd been there. I had lived a life of guilt and fear and, now that I was back, I was more than ready to enjoy life! I discovered that I had friends living in the nearest city to Joy. And when I say "friends", I mean that I met them on an aeroplane once. They were awesome. I got to know my family better too, without fear. And I accepted life as an adventure instead of a chore to be endured.

I used Warmshowers to find a place to stay on my journey west. If I had known that I had friends living in the area I was headed for, I wouldn't have bothered. But I did need to meet the van der Wals.

In the Netherlands you don't have to ask what time dinner is, it's always promptly at 18:00. So, even though I wasn't certain if I should be joining for dinner, I sent a message to let them know I would be late. I wasn't sure exactly what I was cycling into. I had used Warmshowers a handful of times in Australia, with mixed results. In Europe though... Well, I was about to find out.

I parked my bike and was given a tour of the farm and the school before AJ asked if I was hungry. I was starving because you are always starving when you are cycle-touring, but I played it cool. We gathered some produce from the garden and I threw in a measly selection of things from my pack and sat down to let the family watch me devour it. AJ was just back from America. Like me, he couldn't sit still for very long and the allure of what lay around the corner always kept him adventuring. We traded stories while his family's eyes bulged in disbelief. In turn, I was given a history of Friesland, the language and its culture. It was a late night laced with great conversation and company.

AJ cycled me to the Dutch engineering masterpiece that is the Afsluitdijk. And when we met another cyclist at the junction, he took the new guy home for coffee and a shower while I pedalled for Amsterdam. AJ had been given so much on his recent adventures that he was overjoyed to be giving back. I had learned so much about myself in the weeks that had just passed, that I was overjoyed to be having "family time." Even if it was not my own[25].

Gen met me with smiles and hugs. I heard so many good things about her from the big schooner that I had met in the Kiel Canal that there was no way I could not meet her. The South African Brit was now a permanent resident of the Netherlands and she and her family buzzed with life and love. We shared stories, food, laughs and wine, and I was home. The Netherlands was cold and flat. But it did feel like home.

And I got deeper and deeper into the sense of belonging as I met more of my family. Michella and Tim reminded me that Gerdings are amazing. They may have been from the same country, but they had met in Australia more than a decade earlier. Both had life, travel and adventure pulsing through their blood. And their kids followed their examples.

It's amazing how many things you forget until you get reminded about

---

[25] Yet, they were later to adopt me as a surrogate child, but that is a whole different story.

them by the people with whom you shared the adventures. Travelling down memory lane, you grasp how much you have already enjoyed and endured. You don't realise how far you have come until you are back where you were with new eyes. This was my emotional journey through Jairo in Utrecht. Laurence in Leiden. Jean Michel in the tiny village of Lage Zwaluwe. And Hugo in Breda. All avid adventurers whom I had shared laughs, beers and the pushing of limits with, in distant lands.

There were more family friends to meet up with in Dordrecht. Jenny and I had grown up together but our lives had veered in very different directions. She was now a mum and a doctor. Apart from that, not much had changed, she was still a smiling heart of goodness. But the weather did change.

    I hurried up and finalised my plans. It was October and getting colder fast. My final stop was Daisy, my former flatmate. We'd been housemates the first time that I tried to live in Cape Town. Meeting his wife, Jenna, was long overdue. After hugging them hello, I booked a flight. And then, in a mild panic, I put a quick advert up. I sold my trusty bicycle the following day. I was sad to part with it, but my heart was full and my hug quota was met. Before I knew it, I was headed for the airport and on my way to new adventures.

UNEMPLOYMENT LOOKS BETTER WITH A TAN

15

Larry

B*eing an alcohol-free flight*, my fellow passenger, now friend, and I decided that we had better find a drink at the airport before we parted ways. It was also in keeping with my country visit traditions, even if it wasn't a new country to savour. Did you know that the airport in Johannesburg does not serve beer before ten a.m.? They don't even make exceptions for gypsies that have been gone for months and just survived an alcohol-free flight.

It was scary landing back in my homelands. For the first time in my life, nobody was waiting for me at the airport as my family was all out of town. So, instead of staying in Johannesburg, I caught a bus to Potchefstroom.

"Buy me a cold drink!" demanded a security guard while I waited.
"Um, no."
He sat giving me scary looks for the hour I waited for my bus. And

UNEMPLOYMENT LOOKS BETTER WITH A TAN

there was much more waiting still to come. The bus was not as direct as advertised and I had a few more stops to go. "Expert penis enlargement," read the first sign I saw as I exited the station. There was so much dirt. So much poverty. It was such an adjustment coming from the clean organization of Europe. Was this still my home? Still my country? Or was this the start of me letting go and looking for a new place to properly call home?

I had told my family that I would find my own way to their house, but I had totally underestimated how hot it would be and how complicated it would be lugging 30 kg of stuff uphill. My cousin and grandmother smothered me in hugs. My aunt was at work and my uncle was sitting waiting for me at the wrong bus station. Clear communication is another lesson I am still learning. And even more importantly, actually asking for help.

I smiled looking around the dinner table at all the love that was engulfing me. And I continued smiling all through the week and all the way to Cape Town. I'd been about to take a seat on the bus when somebody waved me to the back of the bus. Did I know these boys?

"We remember you from the plane!" said the smiliest one.

How had they recognised me, I wondered? Was it maybe the giant teddy bear? Or maybe the fact that I was wearing the exact same colourful clothes, underwear included? (All freshly washed of course). We'd travelled from Amsterdam together and were only meeting now. They filled the first five hours of the bus ride with excellent conversation and then hopped off in Kimberly. Nobody goes to Kimberly.

The remaining hours were filled with Jackie Chan movies and conversations with God. What was I doing? What new chapter was I stepping into?

For the first time in bussing history, the bus arrived earlier than scheduled and I wasn't sure what to do at five o'clock in the morning. I broke my number 1 rule and got an Uber. Jeandrés flatmate had decorated the whole apartment with "welcome home" signs for my return.

I spent the day catching up with people and enjoying the speed and mobility my scooter gave me. I ran through the mountains, swam, danced, and got hit by a car on my way to yoga. They were just leaving their class and had clearly transcended to some other level of consciousness. Fortunately, it was just my mirror that cracked and I had a whole hour of heavy breathing ahead of me to relax and unwind. And then my yacht course began.

    I didn't need any qualifications yet, but I had a sneaky feeling that I would be needing them soon, so I used the last of my UK funds to do my STCW[26]. The first half was pure awesome. Our first-aid instructor was so entertaining that I actually enjoyed the course. And the firefighting section was both phenomenal and challenging. But then life turned sour. My first day of Personal Safety and Social Response started with a flat tyre. So, instead of scootering, I cycled there through some of Cape Town's slums. A couple of days later, with a repaired scooter, I swerved for a pedestrian and crashed straight into the back of a car. The worst pain however was enduring Philemon's lessons, he was that boring.

I drove out to meet Larry at last. He had just landed in Cape Town and his boat was finally back in the water. Now he was getting the final things ready for his crossing. I had been speaking to Larry for the greater part of a year. He had first wanted sailing help for the Indian Ocean crossing, but his timing had been less than ideal for both of us and he had paid a crew to deliver the boat to Cape Town instead. We had kept in contact and I had enjoyed laughing and chatting with the helicopter pilot over the telephone. We'd had several recent chats and eventually, I had agreed to meet him and take it from there. He had offered to pay for my flight back to South Africa, but I had opted against it after the terrible episode with Marcus. I did not want to feel like I owed him anything.

    The first time I met Larry in person made me appreciate that. He was not what I was expecting and something inside my gut told me not to do it. I wasn't sure if it was me just having an off day so I helped him with his supply shopping and got his boat in order while I finished my STCW. By the end of it and a night spent on the boat, I could pretend no more. I had to give him an official "no". Paid or not, I was not comfortable spending months alone with him all the way through to Argentina.

---

[26] Standards of Training, Certification and Watchkeeping. The most basic of yachting courses that every person working on a boat, no matter their role or what type of vessel, is required to have.

I think I made a good call. Larry had two false starts and plenty of engine problems on his route. And the crew that did end up helping him is no longer in contact with him.

My STCW finished and I was left with no plans at all. My head hurt with indecisiveness. After a bicycle crash and another scooter crash, I was sure I had somehow stepped outside of God's will. I'd even destroyed my "Life proof" camera in the process of destroying myself. What was I doing in Cape Town? What was I doing with my life?

Bandaged and broken I still somehow managed to clamber up Table Mountain to celebrate the end of my STCW with my crew. They were all excited to head back to and onto the boats they had come from. I was staring at a tabula rasa with no idea what to write.

16

Stepping out onto the Water

Which *brings me to the present. Sat in the lounge room listening to an array of strange melodies. I want to run, but my body is too broken. I want to shower, but Jeandré is still sleeping so I can't get my towel. I want hugs, but I am too dirty. I need a job, but I have no idea what I want to do. I also need to finish writing my book, but I have no idea how to afford it. It's exciting times in gypsy living. What do I really want?*

I went for a job interview to be a waitress. I had never waitressed before in my life, but the woman took one look at me and told me that I was overqualified. I applied to work on a boat sailing around Southeast Asia but they too decided that I was over-qualified.

I became a little bipolar and over-excited about all the things I *might* do and all the places I *might* go. The next moment I would be curled up in a fetal position believing I could do nothing and was worthless. It's the worst place to be stuck adrift – in a sea of uncertainty.

When you stop focusing on your problems, it's amazing how much fun you can have. You start appreciating the good people in your life. You enjoy the mountains. You marvel at the oceans. You laugh so hard that your stomach hurts and before you know it you are back in shape simply by enjoying life. Also, once you let go of trying to steer your own reigns, you allow God to take over.

After an evening run in the mountains, I opened up my laptop to find two emails:

Hi Adeena

How much would it cost for you to transport a boat from Savannah to Sydney harbour?

Greg

...

Hi Adeena

I only have a non-paying position to offer on my sailing yacht - 38' ketch rigged Bermudan cutter, steel. First from Cape Town to Walvis Bay leaving at the end of November '17, then to the Caribbean but back across the North Atlantic in May '18 to Portugal for the Boom festival end of July '18, possibly the Med, then back to the Caribbean through Panama, and zigedy zagedy around the world for five to ten years. No commitments, you can jump off anywhere, and I pay for everything needed for the boat including food and diesel. I'm the official skipper/owner, but all work is shared on the basis of passion and need.

Interested?

Kind regards
Friedrich

I went to bed dreaming of the ocean and I realised how much I missed it.

I replied to Greg to ask how long the delivery would be, what they expected from me, and for more details on the boat and the time frame. When it emerged that they planned to cross the Pacific Ocean in 15 days and thought that they could have an average speed of 26.8 knots, I started to smell some fish. And when the response to my response came back with: "Don't worry about responsibilities, we can work that out when you get here." I decided to give it a miss.

It was a sunny Tuesday when I took the scenic drive out to Hout Bay and parked outside the Mariner's Wharf. I was hit by a flood of flashbacks. I had last visited as a child when I had come to Cape Town on a family holiday. I scanned the area for the man I was meant to meet.

"Five minutes," he signalled as he walked anxiously back and forward pacing militantly while seeming to be everywhere and nowhere.

I wasn't so sure about him.

"Adeena!"

I heard the smile approaching from behind. I spun around to see Friedrich and his daughter and sighed, I'd had the wrong guy.

Friedrich sounded like a nice guy so I thought I would at least pay him the courtesy of a visit. I was humouring myself by doing it. There was no way I was actually going to accept his proposal. The vessel was big and it was blue. It was home-built by a South African woman who had furnished the interior with items that she had collected at second-hand shops. *Arabella* didn't look like much initially, but she had a soul. I nodded and smiled as Friedrich prodded around showing me stuff and pointing at things. I was half listening as my mind silently sprinted in a multitude of directions.

Life is a sequence of choices. And it doesn't matter the magnitude of the decision, we need to get into good habits of choosing what we really want or need. There is no way we can be everywhere at once. Unfortunately, we can't have everything. I'm trying to learn to make decisions purposefully and with unwavering certainty. Sometimes we leap. Sometimes we keep our feet grounded. Sometimes we find ourselves drifting back across the Atlantic. Déjà vu. Life is a series of déjà vus. Someone once told me that insanity is doing the same thing over and over again and expecting different results. I find the contrary. I find that there are always different results. It's not the play-it-safe ones, but the insane ones that will change the world. I didn't mind being labelled "insane".

Originally, we were meant to be leaving on the upcoming Friday. But Friedrich agreed for me to wait my birthday out and hang around for a few extra days. My birthday served as a leaving party too. And, when there were still further delays, there were more leaving parties as we were always on the brink of departure. I went broke in the waiting and had to sell my trusty scooter. It was a sad departure but I needed the cash and I didn't know when I would be back again. Vehicles don't do well when they simply sit and rust. Nothing does.

Instead, I cycled to Hout Bay every day to work on the boat and got fit very quickly while enjoying the picturesque views. Christmas came and, because we were meant to have been gone already, I had to crash other families' parties as mine was off celebrating in Johannesburg without me. I cried a lot, not because I was alone on Christmas, but because of how much God had blessed me with. I was poor, but man was I ridiculously rich!

ADEENA GERDING

PiRaTe QueeN

UNEMPLOYMENT LOOKS BETTER WITH A TAN

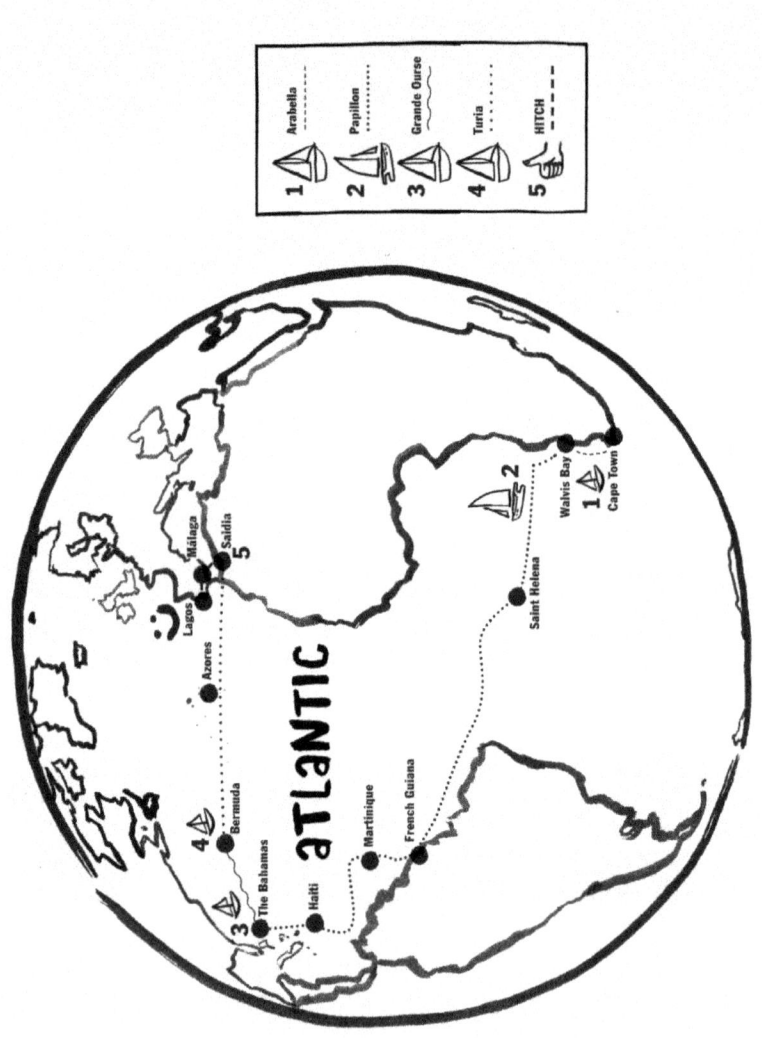

17

Arabella

The seas have calmed to a steady swell. *The wind has set into a Southerly breeze and the seals are merrily escorting us up the west coast of South Africa. We are Namibia-bound at last. Six weeks ago, when I was still 32, I was prepared for this. Both mentally and physically. And my finances were even in better shape. But today, as we're bobbing up and down on these waves, waiting for the potential defrosting of the sun, I wonder. I'm wondering how and why I got here. Why did I let Cape Town go? The most beautiful city in the world, and I'm leaving just as summer begins. The closer we got to leaving, the deeper my connection with the beautiful humans around me became.*

How did I stay on board through all three engine breakdowns? Do I need drama to keep me interested? And then the sudden bureaucratic change in South Africa's maritime rules as we were leaving. God gave me plenty of opportunities to hop off this boat!

How many farewells did I endure? Five? Six? Ten? I drew so many people closer to me than I've had in a long time. I actually allowed myself to form attachments. I even allowed myself to feel. I allowed my heart to beat. Did I leave because I was afraid that people would see the real me? Or did I leave because I needed to?

There was no way I would still be around to welcome Mary Anne to Cape Town. I was there. There was no way I'd be able to show the Swedes around Cape Town. I was there. How good was it to lead them up Table Mountain in the pouring rain? And to show them "my" spots. Why didn't I get to know Stacy earlier? Why did Jeff wait till my last week to ask me out?

But here I am, Sea Gypsy. Arabella *and Friedrich and Tim and me and the deep blue sea.*

We failed to leave Hout Bay because we had a burst water pipe. And when we finally did, there was a loud thunk and the engine seized up. The anodes? The shaft? We sailed into the Royal Cape Yacht Club and missed immigration a second time. Friedrich feared the worst. I was right though; it was simply kelp stuck in the propeller.

Seven hours out I could still see my old home. It was as if I were meant to stay. Swim back? Grow up? I fought the pangs of loneliness that had already started stabbing me.

Yesterday, when the wind vane seized up and we had to start hand steering, the hand steering made me homesick for Yoldia. *And I pined for Karl. This is going to be an emotional leg, but let the tears come. Let the old out to make space for the new. Let go Adeena. Let go and let life unfold.*

With $300ish[27] to my name and that teddy bear, this is the least I have ever left home with, but I am trusting that it is all going to be okay. Looking at that sunrise, it just might be.

---

[27] In an assortment of currencies.

Fresh supplies were dwindling. The boat was rocking like a seesaw. Indecisive waves were hitting us from all directions. Sleep was out of the question. We were on the wrong tack, so every time I dozed off, tools would miraculously fly and cupboards would expel all of their contents. And as soon as it calmed, someone would drop a lone cup in the sink and it would ricochet about like gunfire in a war zone. Or the captain would try some new steering technique that was destined to fail. Psychologist, Actuary, musician, and inventor. I hated all of these professions he claimed to be. Right then all I wanted was humans.

Tim was aboard because regulations had changed and we were not allowed to leave the country without a fully licensed skipper. Tim was human. At 74, Tim didn't give a shit what anyone else thought. He was real and more full of life than most of the teenagers I have ever met. I loved him like a brother. The captain hated him.

Tim cooked dinner but once before he was dispelled from the galley. His Parkinson's left a mess. But who puts carpets in a kitchen anyway? Especially on a boat? And there was no chance the captain was cooking because he was too busy inventing. Also, his idea of cooking was eating tuna out of a can or cured vegetables from a sachet. Normally, sailing gives you plenty of time to write and be creative, but our captain wanted to test every single one of his sails in every manner of configuration. So we were hand steering for eight hours each, dancing with the sails for a few more and then laying down too angry to sleep. Conditions could have been worse I suppose.

It had been another wakeful night when I clambered into the cockpit. I found Tim fuming. He had thrown his mug overboard because Friedrich made him cold coffee. He actually liked that mug. He was more than ready for bed when I took over the watch.

"This is sailing and sailing is meant to be fun." I decided at 4:46 a.m. on that starless morning while sat on the tiller with no music for distraction. I proclaimed the day "a great one". Friedrich was late for his watch; no matter, it was going to be a great day. I went inside to make pancakes because how can any pancake day not be spectacular? But I got a yell from the cockpit as I was still making the coffee that I needed to give me the boost to find the energy to make pancakes. The genoa halyard had broken. I turned off the stove and ran out to help. But I shouldn't have rushed. Friedrich was simply staring at it trying to defuse the best way to solve the problem. The coffee water was cold when I returned and pancakes were delayed, but it didn't matter, it was a great day. I was just trying to decide which oil to use when the boat heeled and coated the countertop with pancake ingredients - a mix of flour, eggs, and goo everywhere. I removed the anti-skid tablecloths and cleaned everything. I started again with Friedrich telling me that our trip was delayed on my account.

"We'll wait for you Adeena. Don't worry."

I forced a smile and fried the boys' pancakes, even taking the time to add cheese because, as I may have mentioned, it was a great day.

"It's too salty," said the captain.

"I'm full," said Tim.

So, I sat down and ate mine while they watched me. I decided to have another one because I had been up since 3:53 am and dreaming of pancakes since six. But I knew they were waiting so I ate too quickly and entered the cockpit feeling rather queasy.

I waited more than an hour for Friedrich to get his tools together and fix the wind vane. But that's okay, I had only two more goals for that great day: finish cleaning everything and have a nap. We fixed the wind vane problem with Friedrich gracefully hanging off the stern. And then proceeded in the slowest sail change in history because it had to be perfect and perfection takes too much thinking. Friedrich successfully skipped hand steering for his entire watch and when Tim took over, he discovered there were other problems with the autopilot and our woes were all but over. It was shaping up to be a great day indeed.

I finished cleaning the kitchen. I washed the anti-skid and all my scummy clothes. I washed myself and the dishes and then made more pancakes for lunch. By 14:47 I lay down with the satisfaction that all my goals for the great day may actually be achieved, it was nap time. But it was 15:03 when Friedrich had me get up to get blocks out from underneath me. Still a great day. Even if I'd never troubled him to get anything out from under his bed, where all my possessions were currently living. A few minutes later, my alarm told me to head to the cockpit for my watch. Friedrich sat there staring at the blocks that he had urgently needed. I was not sold on the sail-to-tiller contraption he was scheming. I'm an optimist and a believer. But there are limits.

We were lost in a sea of beautiful fishing boats. Birds decorated the sunset before the beauty got smothered by a cloudy mess. Friedrich eventually arrived for his watch and I escaped to the warm indoors to prepare dinner. Well-sated and ready for sleep, I waited until the last minute for anyone to offer to do the dishes. I gave up and did the third batch for the day. I felt so angry that I offered the boys coffee instead of speaking my mind. Angry and fuming I crawled onto the couch that doubled as my bed. Diesel fumes hit my head like a hammer. I mentioned it and was returned with the rundown on the compound leak and how only one drop of diesel is being lost every hour and…

"What a lovely smell," I replied.

I turned over and smothered my face with a cushion to mask the fumes and come to terms with the fact that I may have gotten my days confused.

"Today was not a great day, today was shit."

Six years later (Which was really only nine days in human time) we sailed into Walvis Bay, Namibia. Well, we motored in, in actuality. Crew morale was at an all-time low and mutiny was on the cards. Friedrich wanted to play with sail contraptions to guide us through the windless runway of flamboyant seal colonies. We made him turn on the engine. When the wind whispered, "hello", he murdered the engine and we slowly progressed at 1.2 knots. We had only 12 miles to go, but that was going to take at least forever.

We perfectly tidied up the boat before the captain deemed it ready, and we could finally chug into the anchorage under the last of the setting sun. Friedrich reminded me that if we had not tidied up the sails perfectly, we would not have been able to enjoy the sunset from the bow. I almost pointed out that we were the only boat in the anchorage and we could cause dangerous physical harm to him and there would be no one around to see it. Then we could have enjoyed an even more perfect sunset from the mooring with a beer….

It was hard work grabbing the mooring ball with a Friedrich contraption. And there was far too much overthinking for such a simple manoeuvre.

"Beer o'clock!" I called as we finally shut down the engine.

But Friedrich had other thoughts, and instead, we launched the dinghy. We were going to find his mum and go out for dinner.

"I'm not coming," said Tim, which kind of ruined the idea of celebrating crew dinner.

But Friedrich assured me I still needed to come. Or at least that was the plan until he tried rowing the little sailing dinghy for the first time. She was a *sailing* dinghy. She was not built for rowing. I was quite happy to have the evening in and, of course, a beer.

Tim and I hitchhiked ashore in the morning to savour the flavours of land. We may have wandered in the wrong direction, but it was far too pretty to get upset about and we earned our ice-creams by the time we finally found the town. Connected to the internet again, I discovered that I hadn't missed much. I felt like I had been gone a lifetime, but for everyone else, life had simply gone on.

We waited for ages to go back to *Arabella*. Eventually, Friedrich rowed himself in and Tim and I returned home for dinner and too much travel talk. I forced him to go to bed at 23:30 and then spent the night awake, trying to find rest.

A couple of days later, I could take the inner turmoil no longer and I decided to confront my skipper about it. The words came out a bit too quickly without any processing and I am not sure I voiced them correctly. But two important things were said:
1) Friedrich was taking all the fun out of sailing.
2) He corrected and belittled me to the point that I felt like a retard, so I had stopped talking to him (except to answer him) four days earlier.

He hadn't noticed.

He wasn't ready for my confrontation either and threw back:
"Well, for someone who has sailed so much, you should at least know how the wind works."

"Friedrich, I am not the one who claims to be Jesus. You could have organised the perfect wind and walked on the water."

And then we jousted, hurling loaded insults at each other's hearts.

All out of meanness, we sat silently until Friedrich suggested we wait a couple of days to let it blow over before we talk about it any further.

He climbed ashore and I suddenly looked at the currents engulfing us. I was going to be rowing back to Arabella alone.

"I'm not a very good rower," I admitted.

I would be rowing into the wind against the current in a little boat that hadn't reincarnated into quite the right form. Friedrich started giving me a lesson on the wind and the currents so I simply pushed off to stop myself from hurling any more disrespect in his direction. I was being dragged in the wrong direction very quickly, so I rowed harder. If we'd had real oars and oarlocks, I may have made it. I got close and then started drifting towards the rocks.

"FLIP! GOD, HELP!" I cried out.

I decided to grab onto a nearby catamaran and loosened up the sinking paddles to avoid scratching it, but I did it too early and missed. Now, there was no way of avoiding a collision with the break wall.

I jumped out to save the brunt of the dinghy on the rocks but slipped. I was carrying my laptop, all my electronics, and both of my passports. I almost lost it all in one fall.

I pushed the dinghy away holding its painter while I placed my precious possessions on a safer rock then tried to carry the fibreglass dinghy up. I cut my legs up in the process, but I needed to save the dinghy. The flipping *sailing* dinghy. Friedrichs' flipping *sailing* dinghy. Half of me wanted to be badly hurt so he could understand what an asshole he had been. But travel insurance is such a hack. And my mum would miss me if I were gone. I suddenly missed my mum.

A truck drove past before I could completely destroy myself. Three men hopped out and lifted both me and the boat to safety. They dressed my wounds and gave me beer. They drove me and the boat back to the yacht club shelter and made sure I was good before they returned to work. I was reminded once more how much God loved me. I plonked myself next to the BBQ and decided I would wait for the current to swing before attempting it all again.

Two days later, Tim and I drove out of Walvis Bay. The simple idea of leaving the boat filled me with so much joy that I had the first actual night of sleep that I'd had in weeks. Of course, the adventure didn't begin nearly as smoothly as we had envisioned. But that's simply because Friedrich assured us that we needed a four-by-four and had tried to micromanage Tim's adventure. Tim wandered off out of hearing distance to avoid getting violent. Tim wouldn't harm a fly, but a Friedrich was another story.

We explored caves and valleys and sand dunes and canyons. Tim's passion for the bush enhanced the adventure and his good vibes reminded me how good it was to be alive. Suddenly I was singing and dancing again. Enjoying life. I had forgotten what it felt like to enjoy life. I had forgotten how good it felt to smile. I'd forgotten what happiness was. The animals danced around us as we moved through the country. We adopted a small Brazilian child at some point. His dad had twisted his ankle and we seemed responsible enough company to be trusted. What a weird rigmarole of people. A perfect patchwork of vivacious explorers.

꙳

Normally, pilgrims progress to some sacred ground or holy place. But the dinghy battles simply carried me to floating purgatory. Returning to *Arabella* was even harder than it had been before. It resembled a prison. It was owned by a dictator. And losing Tim was like losing the last remnants of life. Tim had kept his side of the bargain, he had given us the legal requirement to leave South Africa. His work aboard *Arabella* was done and he returned to Cape Town.

"If you were so unhappy, why did you smile so much?" Friedrich asked.
    He told me that I was a chronic guilt tripper and a liar.
    "If your friends haven't told you that, they aren't real friends."
    We weren't doing particularly well at diffusing our crewing problems. On the way back from returning the rental car, I was given a scientific explanation of how to use the vacuum cleaner. Once more I rowed back in a huff. I called a few friends to check if Friedrich was right. And while they assured me that I was just fine the way I was, the nails were already holding me on my cross. Alone on the boat, I collapsed into tears. Why had I left Cape Town for this? Why was I here? The blue moon spring tide decorated the anchorage with jellyfish corpses.

Three weeks later we still hadn't left Namibia nor sorted out our differences. I felt worthless and useless, so I worked as hard as I could to somehow give value to *Arabella*. Friedrich stayed ashore with his mother. He visited the boat simply to leave more work for me, create havoc, and construct new devices that would somehow cause me much physical and emotional damage. He seemed intent on sucking my soul dry like a vampire. The worst part is that I let him.

I sat aboard one of the neighbouring boats and watched the crew laugh and smile and have fun. Fun, I had forgotten what it was. Tim had been the last resemblance of it. I'd shared plenty of beautiful moments with other crews as I had waited for the currents to change. There was always someone to laugh with or learn from or help. But then I would be locked away in *Arabella* again, my prison of despair. Tears. Worthlessness.

I was still sitting on a neighbouring boat when my phone rang.

"Adeena, can you…" Friedrich rattled off a long list of things he wanted me to do.

"I can," I replied, "but we still haven't had our chat and I am still not sure that I will be sailing with you."

"Are you alright?" asked Lynn.

I had suddenly descended from Adeena to the inmate. She topped up my wine glass and hugged me. Funny, for catamaran people, the crew aboard *Papillon* were remarkably real.

"We're almost tempted to steal you," they laughed as I clambered into the dinghy and wobbled my way back to *Arabella*.

I needed the run to sweat all the alcohol from my body. Also, the following day was finally set to be leaving day so there was no way I could simply sit on the boat. I cried out to God in the desert as I took shelter under the only tree, a garbage heap from all the predecessors who had stolen its shade.

"Where are you, God? Why? What do I do?"

I cried and cried and cried.

I wanted love. I wanted community. I wanted life. I was tired of feeling like a slave. And I was so broke that I felt like I didn't have any other option. But I was going to talk to Friedrich soon and I had to say something. I opened up the Bible app on my phone when my waterfalls were allowing my eyes to see once more.

Psalm 113:7-8
He lifts the poor from the dust and the needy from the garbage dump.
He sets them among princes, even the princes of his own people!

I ran back and dived into the cold shower. I was late to meet my skipper, but it was perfect timing and I was ready. We spoke through everything and, by the time we reached the dinghy, we had worked a lot of things through.

"Better to end in pain than to have never-ending pain."

We sat down in the cockpit to laugh about some of our miscommunications and misunderstandings. When I had told Friedrich I was on a journey to find myself again after so many years of travelling and living other people's lives, he had thought I was asking for his help. I was not, it was a discovery I really had to make for myself. Friedrich had intended to sail single-handed but his family had worried about him and talked him out of it. He dreamed of fiddling and inventing. I wanted freedom and adventure. We had very different objectives and it was clear that there was no possible way we could share the boat. I was also not ready to go back to Cape Town because I wanted to move forward, not backwards. Besides, flights to Germany were cheaper than buses to Cape Town anyway.

I was sitting in the cockpit busy booking my ticket to Germany and wondering where best I might have the chance to find a job when the neighbours dinghied up.

"Do you want to come with us?" they asked.

"Sure," I replied because I thought they were simply going to the supermarket.

The next thing I knew, I had agreed to jump ship and sail across the Atlantic with them. They were leaving in an hour.

18

Papillon

Papillon *was a beautiful boat.* I'd been aboard only once prior for some drinks with the crew. The four of them were awesome, even if they had oversaturated me with alcohol. Lynn and Todd were American. They both had grown-up kids from previous marriages, but in each other, they had found their soul mates. They had decided to make a restart in Florida. They gave up "real life" because it wasn't for them. Instead, they decided to get a boat as a home. They had searched America for the perfect boat and failed to find it. But they did find one online and had travelled halfway around the world, to South Africa, to get it.

Tiaan was hired locally as a captain. He was newly qualified and this was his first ocean crossing but he was a sharp Boer with loads of gumption. He had asked if he could bring his girlfriend with him. And so,

Selina joined the crew too. Her Irish lustre added something dynamic to the arrangement.

They had sailed up the coast of South Africa and cruised past all the beautiful spots I had missed on *Arabella*. They were happy and full of life and the contrast could not have been more dramatic. The boat felt like a 56-star retreat. I did have to grow my sea legs all over again with the motion of the catamaran though, and nausea was ever-present, but it was still good. Everything about it was good.

I messaged Karl to tell him that I had sold my soul to a catamaran. He was far from a priest, but I needed to confess my sins to someone who understood the gravity of the situation. I had spent many years mocking catamaran people. I saw them as a lower creed of vessel [and sailor], like bicycles with training wheels. Karl assured me that I would be alright, unless it was a *Lagoon*.

"You should have gone with the European escape instead," he said.

And then reminded me that I was long overdue for a visit.

"It's too cold," I replied.

"It's okay, we have beer…. And you can always cuddle."

I suddenly missed him immensely and wondered what it would be like sailing with two couples. Fortunately, they were both lovely. And even more fortunately, it was not a Lagoon, but an Admiral 38. *Papillon* was equipped with three cabins and two heads. Lynn and Todd lived on the portside while the rest of the crew shared the other hull. Tiaan and Selina were in the aft cabin and me and Teddy in the fore cabin.

We sailed off into an exquisite sunset with the wind working with us. The catamaran cruised straight past Friedrich and *Arabella* and on to new adventures as my past faded away and my smile grew. How quickly plans change. We are always where we need to be.

My stomach churned with the new motion of the boat and I spent the first hours huddling with a bucket. I couldn't sleep because I had to get accustomed to the slapping sound that the waves caused on the hull. Still, you couldn't possibly wipe the smile off my face!

We spent the day tacking up the Skeleton Coast and while Selina and I both battled to keep food down, a big braai was being prepared and there was no way we were skipping those lamb chops! The stars seemed to sparkle brighter and the air aboard was so much fresher on *Papillon*. She was immediately home.

We anchored for a swim and a sea-shower. The seals danced around us and life was perfect. And, after an afternoon basking in the beauty of the nothingness, it really was time to go. We raised the anchor and turned West to cross the Atlantic.

I ran to wake the captain; he had a fish on his line. We watched in awe as the battle ensued: man vs fish. It lasted over an hour as we glided through the bluest of Atlantic blues under a maroon spinnaker. We stood ready with nets, cameras and appetites. But… what was it exactly? The strangest-looking fish came in. Was it pregnant? Was it a puffer? We all shot each other uneasy glances before Tiaan freed the line and sent the fish back. We returned to being mesmerized by the oceany blues. We munched watermelon instead of sashimi and let the peels race each other off the transom.

By dusk, we had another catch. Fish was back on the menu! We all took up our places and watched Tiaan reel in a shark. It thrashed and writhed until we cautiously freed it. The previous day's leftovers weren't too bad as a compromise meal!

I spent Valentine's Day fifth wheeling with two very affectionate, loving couples. Lynn and Todd celebrated their third anniversary and Tiaan and Selina, almost five months. It was probably the first time in my life that I actually celebrated the day. And it wasn't all bad, my heart was so full of love that it seemed appropriate.

Meals got better by the day and I even started appreciating the flying fish corpses I collected off the bow. Deep fried in bread crumbs, they were delicious. It was the first boat since *Yoldia* that I really felt like I belonged on. I hoped that my smile muscles could take it; they were working overtime.

We shared life. We had family meals in the cockpit. We played games. We cooked together and laughed together. Every day was a different stew of goodness.

UNEMPLOYMENT LOOKS BETTER WITH A TAN

DAY 9, Sunday 18 February: The morning is a beautiful glow of blue-blue Atlantic depths and sunshine. Flying fish are racing past. Coffee has just been brewed and cherry chocolate rusks are being opened. My handline is out and I'm a bit sceptical seeing as most of the shiny stuff has already rubbed off my lure. But I have good faith that fish will be served today. We are making four knots again and the day reeks of epic. I just hope it won't end up like Arabella's *"Great Day" because that wasn't all that good.*

I did a morning workout before I made the daily bread. The wind has died a little, but the fish have multiplied and the dorado have hung out with us all afternoon.

By this evening, they even decorated our hooks as both Tiaan and I reeled one in. That's right folks, it's a vis braai naand[28]! And because it was already planned and defrosted, we get rotisserie chicken too! And while I am writing this, potatoes are being mashed and we are selecting a soundtrack worthy of the occasion.

How lucky we are to be alive? How lucky I am to be sailing Papillon, *living the good life!*

We celebrated Lynn's birthday at sea. We'd planned to be on land already, but sailing never goes quite as planned. I took the sunrise watch and had the opportunity to balloon and decorate the boat before having the honour of bestowing the first hug upon her. When in good company everything can be fun and life tastes delicious. In fact, every meal is marinated in love. Time seems to both fly and have no restraints at all because you are simply enjoying the moments; a sommelier with a sensitive palate.

We crossed the Prime Meridian and our celebrations stretched over into the Western Hemisphere. The day was most excellent and as the clock struck midnight, it fell off the wall and shattered. Either the day was not meant to end, or the perfect day was finally achieved. Either way, we didn't want tomorrow to come.

"Land ho," cried Lynn as we finally saw it creeping higher next to the setting sun.

---

[28] Fish BBQ night.

We laughed and feasted and then all plonked on the trampoline to watch both dissolve into stars. At 00:31 we moored in "The most extraordinary place on Earth". I was back in Saint Helena. It's the kind of island most people are lucky enough to visit once in a lifetime, and I was back for a second time.

I was on the loo when I heard a familiar voice. I stumbled up to the deck to see James Herne. I'd first met him and his family in Panama upon *Yoldia*. And then again in Fiji on both *Rewa* and *Yacare*. They'd been docked near Larry's boat in Cape Town. And now there they were, back home, in Saint Helena, where they had come from. When they began their voyage, they had only one kid. They returned with three. I can't imagine a better childhood to gift a kid with than a voyage around the world. With more than enough adventures behind them, they were very ready to settle down and start up their yacht services to help others do the same.

We re-celebrated Lynn's birthday in style and went through all the usual motions. Supplies were bought. Alcohol was consumed. The island was explored. And life was enjoyed. Three days of awesome. It culminated in a sleepless night. Boys were on my mind. Why were the ghosts of my past still haunting me? Why couldn't I just enjoy the simple present and be happy?

I crawled out of bed and into the cockpit where the world was just turning pink before Lynn arose to make blue pancakes. All sorts of boats arrived from Walvis Bay and Cape Town and there was a happy series of hellos and goodbyes. And still no Friedrich. Maybe the past wasn't really trying to catch up to me?

The mooring lines had tangled themselves so badly that a very slow departure ensued. Tiaan and I swam circles around each other trying to untie the knots before we finally watched the land shrink behind us. I was sad to see it go, but I was excited to keep moving. What lay ahead? Yes, we were headed for French Guiana, 1754 miles away, but where would we wash up? Who would be there? Would I find a job? Or do a boat delivery? Would I find love? Or was I predestined to be a lonesome sailor forever?

UNEMPLOYMENT LOOKS BETTER WITH A TAN

19

Neptune be Nice

You forget how big oceans are until you are lost in the middle of them. Your dreams escalate to all levels of crazy and, in our case, the galley produced food so tantalizing that you could barely imagine a life not satiating all of your basic needs. Life was as tasty as it could possibly be. Every day was filled with laughter and adventure and attempts to catch fish (and finish our surplus of jalapenos). Meals were always shared in the cockpit where, being on a catamaran, we could actually put the whole spread and all the condiments out. There was always a spread. And there was always a big selection of hot sauces and cayenne powders.

"Eyes!" called the captain.

We knew the drill, that chilli powder loved to float in the wind and sting the eyes of unsuspecting crew members. It was our version of saying grace.

The wind danced. It blustered and died and changed direction. We were in the trades, but they didn't seem to be working very well. We took turns in swimming off the stern. And the surfboard even came into play a couple of times. We played deck tennis on the trampoline bow. And there was always someone working out somewhere. Such a strange conglomeration of humans, but such a nice one, too. All different, but somehow so similar.

"Cheers!"

We all raised our glasses as we patiently waited. It wasn't just the wind that was out of sync, sometimes the cooking was too. We were having a pizza night to celebrate what was meant to be the 1000-mile mark. The champagne had been chilled too. But we weren't quite there yet. Lynn had offered me ready-made bases but I wanted them to be made from scratch and be filled with chilli and garlic. I didn't intend for them to take five hours…YES! It truly was five hour pizza!

Night-time dreams became a series of fighting off exes from ghost's past. Why did they always come at night? Why were my dreams so vivid and real? Why could I not let them drift into the past like the lands we left when we set sail? Had I made some mistakes? Should I turn back and question them? Or simply let them go?

I was always semi-asleep when I stumbled into the cockpit for sunrise watches. The others did their watches as couples. Being the lone sailor, they always gave me the sunrise as my responsibility. What a blessing!

I had my morning routine. I would do all the checks and with each check came a series of stretches. Then I would put the kettle on while I cleaned and swept the cockpit. Those dark hairs had my DNA all over them. I shook the matt over the stern, something was hanging there. A line? A bucket? I checked, and there was nothing that had fallen off the boat.

"Wow!" I screamed in almost disbelief as the morning sun gave clarity to the situation.

A giant[29] ray was hitching a ride in our wake. The morning was lost in mesmerisement.

"Hey Lynn, take a look down there," I said as I gave her a good

---

[29] 9-10 feet across.

morning hug.

"Holy shit!"

I heard her swear for the first time ever. The others, as they awoke, screamed in joy too. Something so beautiful, so rare! It stayed with us for hours, simply enjoying our boat stream of good vibes.

The kettle was boiled again as we were actually approaching the thousand-mile mark. It was too early for champagne, but Amarula coffee was a win. And Ray, as we named our hitchhiker, was a happy guest for the occasion. So much joy filled the morning but then suddenly there was a lull. I wanted to cry. PMS? Tiredness? No doubt. Or over-awedness? I sat down to write my book because I needed distraction from the present, but I was rewriting about the pirates that Brazil had held and about more past loves, so I put pen to paper instead:

I called this section of my life "Pirate Queen" because I wanted to face my fears and I refused to have them take me over again. But I'm headed straight back to South America and I am terrified! I can't believe that it's been almost five years since I first crossed the Atlantic. And I can't believe how much I have seen and experienced since then. I've grown up so much but still, my head and heart linger in uncertainty. I'm confused, lost, and complexed.

We lost Ray as we tacked. But Selina fried up an excellent dinner and Tiaan began making home-brew. It was an action-packed day, which eventually had me sitting down in silent awe on the trampoline. Was I listening? Did God have something to say?

༄

The days passed and we laughed through games and challenges. When the generator was running, we all ran to charge devices and write and edit various projects on our computers. When there was no power, we would use our hands to craft things or write on paper or work out. We were always busy with nothing in particular or particularly busy with everything particular. But we were still human and still had to deal with our own insecurities and needs. I stood in the kitchen preparing dinner, feeling completely unworthy of so awesome a crew. I broke the bowl with my brute force and over-spiced the dish. I felt like a waste of time and space. I felt like I had nothing to offer. I felt like I was in the way. I felt...

"Dolphins!" came the cry from the cockpit.

And we all ran to the deck to see them living their destiny. It was amazing how much such a simple thing could restore me. But also, what was my destiny? Why was I here? I couldn't sleep, so I lay awake praying for other people.

We weren't moving quite as quickly as we had hoped and there were definite concerns regarding how much food and, more importantly drinking water, we had left. There had been a lot of optimistic talk thrown into coercing Lynn to do the ocean crossing. Time scales and risks were downplayed. It worked, but seeing as Lynn had been the one who had done most of the provisioning, it was a little concerning. My presence aboard didn't make it any easier seeing that there were now five mouths to feed rather than the four that had been provisioned for. We ate a lot of lentils and rice, but meals were still of a culinary standard that is hard to describe on paper.

I joined a marching band. Or at least it was a band that marched. We were in it purely for the travel perks and for the free stuff. We were eventually busted for being fraudulent, but we were given a chance to prove ourselves. We rapped a set of songs about white and brown chocolate and were pulling it off very well until someone started drumming out of tune. I searched the room trying to find the culprit. It happened again. And then my name rang out, Selina was banging on my door, trying to awaken me for my sunrise watch. At least, for what used to be the sunrise watch. Our clocks needed some adjusting to match the sun a little more correctly.

My body was still waking up when my mind raced into to-do list mode. The coffee wasn't even made yet, and already it was on overload with no off button.

How do I simply turn it off and enjoy the moments? We're so close to land that I'm on overdrive. And when I say "so close" I mean closer to halfway, but still... My skin is breaking out in little blistery boils and my legs are really cramping up. I shudder to think what state I would be in if I had stayed aboard Arabella. *A few more days of Blue Therapy will sort me out.*

Or at least that's what I believed.

"One cannot define nor forecast the conditions that make happiness; one stumbles upon them by chance in a lucky hour at the world's end somewhere."

- Willa Cather

Saint Patrick's Day! Obviously, I was excited, it's the only holiday I celebrate somewhat religiously. The sun rose rather fittingly as I danced on the deck and decorated the boat. We were 19 days out from Saint Helena and a celebration was in desperate need. Selina and I put together an Irish playlist for the occasion. We enjoyed it with a banana bread breakfast, which isn't particularly Irish but is definitely in keeping with the celebratory nature of the day. The homebrew was finally sampled and while it wasn't particularly good, it was definitely alcoholic. The day culminated with dolphins in the afternoon and sailfish in the setting sun as we sipped on champagne. This was a Saint Paddy's Day first, nobody drinks champagne on Saint Patrick's Day.

"To be sure, to be sure," cried Selina.

It sure was a flipping good day!

Rain seemed to be stirring and we were all ready for it. Soap and shampoo in hand, and brooms and brushes at foot. *Papillon* hadn't had a freshwater wash for longer than we hadn't. Only it was a false alarm, so we had a lunch break instead. Another false alarm came with it. That's when we noticed the wind vane was loose. So, instead of a shower, we belayed Tiaan up the mast. He had just about finished securing it when the rains started. A white t-shirt was the least appropriate attire for the occasion[30].

It dripped like honey and then it poured. And the rain was kind enough to stick around long enough for us to scrub both the deck and our bodies as we laughed and sang and danced. Oh, did we laugh.

---

[30] I had long given up wearing underwear.

ODE TO **PAPILLON**

Welcome to **Papillon**, *our floating home.*
Across the Atlantic, we do Roam.

We sail the oceans night and day
Followed closely by a giant Ray.

The spinnaker flares dark blue and red
But occasionally we use the jib instead.
The crew's a mix of some strange creatures
Kiff and awesome, fantastic features.

Tiaan's always creating things
While Selina dances around and sings.
Todd really knows how to chill
While Lynn is in the kitchen preparing our fill.
I drift about and pretend to be busy
While the homebrew sits and tries to go fizzy.

The fish in the sea
Are plentiful and free
Can we get them on the hook?
They won't even look!

The dolphins have visited once or twice
But some whales or orcas would be nice.

The temperature has risen quite a lot
And the humidity increases with every new spot.
We sweat so much, we don't need to shower
So fragrant are we like sweet summer flowers.

Sunrises and sets and shooting stars
Much more beautiful than civilization and cars.

*We're lost in a wonderful world of bliss
But still aiming for land, trying not to miss.*

*Look out French Guiana, we're approaching
The time for cold beer is fast encroaching.*

The sun rose shooting violent luminousness across the sky. It was pancake Tuesday and while they were delicious, their preparation was tainted by false alarms of us sinking and failed attempts to reel in fish. There were also two ginormous vessels on the horizon, making the breakfast celebration a bit of an unsettled one. But the day dissolved into blue with a green curry for dinner. We turned the clock back and carried on inching forward. The sea was wild and my fore cabin bed a rodeo. Sleep was hard to come by as I clung to my mattress tight. At least the phosphorescence through my porthole was spectacular.

There were so many knocks that I eventually got up to check if it was watch time. I was early, but with the clocks being set back, first light was already illuminating the sky. I bid Lynn goodnight. At precisely 6:30 a.m. *Papillon* time, we crossed into the Northern Hemisphere. With the sunrise came a double rainbow. I stared out at the horizon wondering what the North had in store for me this time around, the last time was ridiculous!

Lynn prepared a special lunch to celebrate both the crossing of the equator and Spring Day. The table was decorated with a Lindt tree (Which we will now refer to as a Lynn-dt tree). Out came the pizza, which didn't even take five hours to cook because Lynn is far wiser and much less stubborn than I am. Next emerged five beers. We had long been out and I have no idea where she had been hiding them. I wanted to leap up and hug her, but the sea was raging and all our limbs were carefully holding on to things already spread on the table.

To aid digestion, we read and chilled and enjoyed a half attempt at a shower in the drizzle. Then suddenly, after five days of waiting, nature finally beckoned me. I escaped to the head. Normally I'm the fastest person in and out of the toilet, but not this time. I was in there for a good 45 minutes as my body cleansed itself. I also almost threw up in exertion. I stumbled out to the entire crew standing in applause. Maybe I needed some Northern air to rid myself of things I'd been holding on to?

Being in the Northern Hemisphere, we had some big duties to fulfil and all relocated to the deck after dinner. Paying tribute to Neptune is of dire importance. The crew had already heard how badly it had unfolded for Karl and me on *Yoldia*, and they were not taking any chances! We each took on one of the elements and a cardinal and gave a fitting tribute while Lynn played the sailor.

The following day, the seas continued to rage and both movement aboard and sleep was out of the question. As was fishing, all our lines were bringing in were massive balls of mustard-yellow seaweed. The algae stained the waves. It was an indoor kind of day. The only other mentionable thing was that I finally beat Lynn at arm wrestling! All my workout sessions seemed to be paying off. In celebration, I made us all seaweed soup.

The rains started. And the rains would not stop. My room began to leak. And while Lynn and Todd tried to fix it, I lost the bucket to the ocean. Spirits were low, the crew were tired, irritable and frustrated. When we caught fish, both lines were snapped off by the massive creatures. We had lamb for dinner and it was delicious, but we were living on a rollercoaster with emotions to match. I almost finished editing my *Papillon* video, but I wasn't sure I liked it. And while my book was almost written, I wasn't even sure what story I wanted to tell. It was all too much! I wanted to cry. I was a failure. I was not enough. I didn't deserve such an awesome crew.[31] I turned my head to a movie and tried to suffocate my thoughts.

The cloudy horizon didn't help clear my thoughts. I thought cleaning might. It did not. I changed the name of my book again and sat in a sea of indecisiveness. This was the fourth working title for my book and how to choose? *First We Ate Your Wife. Confessions of a Sea Gypsy. There's a Gypsy in My Garden. Awaiting Forecast.* Was there a better one? I gave up the day's productivity, chakalaka burgers were on the menu. And I guess that was productive: if you don't eat, you die. We enjoyed the meal, but we were all clearly at our wit's end. Still, there were shining lights to the day, especially the brownies. However, they almost

---

[31] The small lies we allow ourselves to believe.

didn't happen because Selina had explicitly asked for two eggs and we had only left her one.

333 miles to go. The toilet broke, again. My bed was soaked, again. We were living in crazy times. It stopped raining, but that's when the tears came.

100 miles out I was fine. I don't think I have ever felt so calm at the end of an ocean crossing. Should I have been nervous? I had no idea what was in store for any of us, but I had complete peace. A plane swooped down over us to inspect the vessel and the marines radioed through to confirm our intentions. It was the first radio call we'd had in months; there was still life out there! But what were we doing in French Guiana?

UNEMPLOYMENT LOOKS BETTER WITH A TAN

20

Frolicking through French Cuisines

Q***uite suddenly our world of blue became green,*** as we chugged up the Maroni River into French Guiana. Birds and bees darted about us as we sat in awe of the rainforest that decorated the riverbanks. Fishermen smiled and waved as we passed. We turned the music off to hear nature buzz its welcome.

We tied up to a mooring and launched the dinghy off the trampoline. Then we took it in turns to have fresh water showers seeing as we had managed to arrive with half a tank to spare. The engine had warmed the water, so it was especially nice. Champagne. A cheer to Neptune, to *Papillon*, to a completed ocean crossing, to life, to the crew, and to Jesus. We'd made it to South America.

Complementary beers awaited us at the yacht club, as did a host of smiling faces. It was a much friendlier arrival than my Brazilian one had been on the previous Atlantic crossing. We explored our way to the restaurant that the yacht club manager had recommended. It felt so good to stretch our legs again. And it was heavenly to sniff at the almost-forgotten scents of land. All sated and exhausted, we dinghied back and drifted quickly off to sleep in our tranquil rainforest paradise.

The market was a dream of colourful fresh goodness. After weeks at sea, we craved raw deliciousness. The town was a mix of Columbian vibes and Guadeloupe beats. It carried a broken-glass third-world vibe, despite it belonging to the first. The population seemed to come from everywhere. We made friends with the yacht club staff and a few people in the laundromat, but otherwise, we remained outsiders, simply sharing smiles.

Despite the heat and humidity, I managed to get a few runs in. I got lost in both wonder and awe (and also tropical deluges). Endorphins made me feel alive again. And life was pulsing through us all in new ways. Especially Selina, suspicions were confirmed, she was indeed pregnant.

It was amazing to reconnect with family and friends around the world. So much and nothing had happened while we had drifted across the Atlantic. Friedrich had eventually left Namibia but had hit a dead whale and was still working out how to get lifted out of the water in Saint Helena. I was exceptionally glad that I wasn't there to witness it.

Our cuisine soared to new heights as we feasted on baguettes and French delicacies. We failed to find Chinatown but did find a burlesque show and there was an easter egg hunt and… I sat in the cockpit alone. The others were all cuddled in bed. And I sat cuddling unsettledness and desire. I suddenly missed people. I missed home. I missed Karl. It's why I don't normally just let myself sit. If you keep running, emotions don't have a chance to catch up. I was reminded that there was a world out there going on without me. And while there is nowhere else I would have rather been right then, I realised that my next chapter needed more. I knew that it was all in God's hands, but I was also a little bit worried that I'd had my full quota of blessings too early in life. The calm of the morning made my thoughts seem too loud.

To sum up the rest of French Guiana and our little brush with South America isn't all that easy. Yes, the rains continued and then stopped. The sun did come out. I skyped Karl and ended up joining the table at his family's birthday lunch. There was no denying that there were still feelings there, on both sides. And both his dad and Colette were egging us on. But would I? Could I? Could we actually make it work? This was the reason for the first sleepless night.

I planned on a morning beer run to Suriname. I needed to cross the river and taste the foreign soil and speak Dutch and drink a beer. But I put my needs aside and got sucked into cleaning and laundry first. And then there was supply shopping and unpacking and immigration. Tiaan and Selina went sightseeing while I stayed home and played Cinderella. And after doing the dinner dishes I escaped to the bow to bawl. Not for any other person, but for me. I make unimportant things paramount. I stop myself from doing the things I really want because I see other people as more important than myself. I'm my own worst enemy and somehow set on self-sabotaging my joy. Tiaan turned on the deck lights and I was caught centre-stage in a sea of tears. I thought I had dealt with all of this already, but the limelight caused some dull shadows to fall. This was the reason for the second sleepless night.

And before I had a chance to contemplate much more, we were underway again. Suriname taunted me for all 15 miles that we straddled her shoreline. I tried to shake it, but I was very disappointed in myself. I turned my back on it and vigilantly scanned the French Guiana coast for monkeys and crocodiles. Even with the current working with us, it was a bumpy ride down the Maroni River. As we were spat back out into the Atlantic, we readied the champagne to celebrate both the ocean and the nearby Ariane rocket launch. With the grey murky weather, we didn't see much of either, but the champagne was fantastic.

With storm clouds staining our horizons and *Papillon* a mad bull racing north towards the Caribbean, sleep was out of the question. As was writing, editing, and workouts. If we didn't need to eat, we would have given up on galley activities too. It was almost impossible to stand, let alone do anything productive. My need for affirmation probably drove the whole crew even crazier. And I didn't have the strength to give it to myself. I was a hazardous load of dynamite ready to implode. So, it's a good thing the stars eventually decided to join our vessel again, four days out. After being awed at their beauty, I finally slept, and that made all the difference.

There were blue skies and flying fish again, but Tiaan's lure was a hungry one. It kept eating mine and we got our fishing lines tangled a couple of times before I decided to throw in the towel. It was a Sunday and we needed fish to roast. I sent my fish-willing vibes to his fancy lure. While we still didn't catch any fish, we all slowly started adjusting to our uncomfortable surroundings. I reattempted a workout on the bow and while it was incredibly challenging and doubled as a "shower," it had me feeling so much better. The stars twinkled so brightly that it seemed that they, too, were celebrating life with us!

It was a rough night, but a beautiful dawn. I finally caught a fish, but the bugger made off with my lure. The streaks of luminous seaweed zebra-ed the ocean in the glow of the rising sun. That night, I sat on the roof of the cockpit watching the lights of Barbados pass by, just as I had years earlier. And I was in a very similar state of not knowing what should happen next. Or when? Or how? *But sitting under the overabundance of stars, I know that God knows and I will leave it in His hands so that I don't have to worry about it. In fact, this time I really am not. What I am worried about is where the joy is. Along with the other fruits[32]. Tomorrow or the next day we will wash up on land again. I have added joy to our provisioning list.*

We sailed straight past Saint Lucia and my mind was flooded with memories from my time aboard *Fiddler*. They stayed with me as we raced past Le Diamant Rock. So many adventures had already taken place in those waters. So many tears had also been shed. It is a strange thing joining lines on the map but coming back a different person than you were the last time.

We dropped the main and furled the jib. On the fifth attempt, our anchor finally held. We dove into the turquoise waters to wash off the rough ride we had all just endured and baptize ourselves into the Caribbean.

𝑓

The warm luminous waters we had anchored in were littered with seagrass. And then fish. As we swam further, the underworld transformed into a magical oasis; the full rainbow of life residing in a tiny patch of ocean.

---

[32] Love, peace, patience, kindness, goodness, faithfulness, self-control.

Turtles! Following them was both fun and challenging. Land excursions were beautifully diverse, too. We wandered through volcanic sands and ruins and goats. *Papillon* had become our teleportation device through different realms.

We got ready to set sail for Haiti, but then we realised what day it was. Not only should you never set off on a passage on a Friday, but definitely not on Friday the 13th! So, we ventured further up the coast of Martinique instead.

The island seemed just as magical as it had aboard *Fiddler*. And there was more than enough to captivate our minds and keep our bodies moving! We danced and swam and sang and snorkelled and explored. And when the watermelon went rotten, we had even more fun perfecting our catty (aka slingshot) skills by trying to pelt it as it drifted off into the abyss. This was essential practice; each crew member had their own catty to use for protection. (The day's practice did highlight my concern for our vessel's weapon of choice).

Just after setting the sails, we feasted on cheese and meat and baguettes. It was going to be a bumpy ride, but we were so ready for it. We were getting closer and closer to The United States and Lynn and Todd were getting increasingly excited about going home. And then the naps began. We were all exhausted. I was tempted to follow the other's lead, but I knew myself better and instead, I opted to go to the "gym". Happy endorphins make everything better. The days spiralled through ocean blues and waves awash with seaweed.

It was a strange land I lost myself in and I had to get creative with payments because I couldn't bring myself to use the local currency. Not because I was broke (for a change), but because dealing out blow jobs was not in my life repertoire. I had signed up to study at the *Academy of Life* and because I didn't do bribes and because I wasn't a big spender, I simply had to get good at Life. Art, music, creativity, making people laugh… I had to be an A student because being a B(J) one was not an option. I was busy discussing my latest artwork with another student and trying to get the other students to stand with me. We had to do something to overthrow our horny dictatorship. We were just about to come to an agreement when Selina came knocking. Over breakfast, Lynn and Todd assured me that there are no US states that use blow jobs for currency, so I would be fine.

UNEMPLOYMENT LOOKS BETTER WITH A TAN

There was only seaweed on my fishing line, again. Selina was bleeding. There was a dead bird with a broken neck on the bow. The following morning, I watched the spinnaker sail tear like toilet paper. Bad things were happening but we weren't going to let the events aboard get us down. Some waterfalls of tears were coming out, but I wanted to keep that joy hovering as near as possible. I tried not to let it be washed away. And I found solace in exercise. It was amazing to work out. To let the sweat wash my body like a baptism. The sea would shoot up unexpected sprays of water through the trampolines to drench us, and you had to be careful if your mouth was open. We called workouts on the bow "involuntary showers." I loved them.

"Land ho!" Came the cry 19 miles out. The discomfort of dawn was transforming into a beautiful show of ocean blues and island greens. As we encroached upon Haiti, the waters shifted through all the shades of turquoise. Paradise. Palms. Perfection. Small sailing fishing boats darted across our path and we danced *Papillon* around the fishing traps and nets. The starboard engine played up and Tiaan spent the morning fixing it. A wave swept over the boat and drenched the port cabin, so Selina and Lynn spent the morning drying mattresses and bilges. Todd steered while I sat on the bow keeping a lookout for all the surprises that lined our path. We breathed a sigh of relief as Île á Vache's anchorage came into view. And with it came the pirogues and dugouts and kayaks. Peter and Kiki and Pipi and Jon-Jon. I stopped hearing the names and sat studying all the faces that had come out to welcome us. We were back in a land of poverty and our mere presence was like parading a mansion through the slums. We were money. They wanted it.

By the time we were ready to anchor, we had so many small vessels clinging to the sides of the boat, that we couldn't. Tiaan was very polite in trying to get them to let go, but they hovered like mosquitos ready to attack again. And we had to swat them away again and again as our anchor failed to hold. Eventually, we simply moved the boat to the other side of the bay where a cluster of other boats seemed to be partying. This time it held.

It was quite the party aboard and we were rather inebriated by the time we headed ashore. The waters were beautiful, the shore was laden with palm trees jutting out of the trash. We enjoyed some local delicacies and tried to ignore the pleas for money from the residents while politely acknowledging their presence. It's a fine line we walked trying to be tourists while simultaneously pretending not to be. We feasted and danced and escaped their reality to our safe, cosy confines aboard *Papillon*. The following morning Tiaan and Selina left early for the mainland while we swam in to explore. We were nervous for them, if the country was anything to go by, the doctors may not be the most hygienic. And the real issue at hand… well… we didn't even want to think about it!

We had a young boy join us ashore and he was very friendly as we walked through the luminous hills and trash-strewn beaches exploring. Such an interesting island, with so many smiles, dirty looks, and laundry. The whole island greeted us with what must be Haitian for "Hello" or, in the local dialect, "Give me one Dollar." We started greeting them in their native tongue. The young boy laughed with us and introduced us to people as we went and our crew grew as we sucked in the views and blues and greens. The crowd disappeared and our friend wanted to go too, he looked at me and asked me for money. I didn't have any. A hat? I didn't have that either. "Give me one dollar," he said again so I greeted him back and started down the hill to catch up with Lynn and Todd. I thought an animal stirred next to me so I whipped around to see it. And a rock landed near my face. And another was hurling towards me. I jumped aside and Lynn and Todd followed suit as we ran. Our new "friend" was pelting us with rocks. We slipped into the forest and were shaking with fear when a hymn arose. Kids suddenly smiled at us and our joy returned. We had nothing with us so we swam home for lunch.

The day was still young and seeing that it was meant to be our only day in Haiti, I decided to do more exploration. I followed my feelings and met a lot of beautiful people who seemed to want to connect for more than just the money I did not have. The dirty potholed roads were filled with old motorbikes and donkeys. The rocks and coves were amazing. My bare feet ached from the broken glass I had trodden on the previous night, but I needed to absorb more of this interesting land. I stuck my head into a little local bar to investigate. A yellow-shirted man tried to get my attention; I kept walking. He called out after me but I ignored him and sped up, however, he caught up.

"Hello," he said in English. "Where are you staying?"

"On a boat," I replied, a bit too nonchalant as I turned to walk away.

He took out a badge. I thought it was a driver's license, but he turned out to be the immigration officer. (Even if the picture didn't quite match the face). I gulped.

"When did you get here?... Which boat are you on?... How long are you staying for?... Catamaran or monohull?"

Seeing as we had opted to skip the bureaucracy of checking in, I tried to change the topic and talked about the States instead. He tried again to lure me into the bar. But I wasn't going in there, I could only keep my wits for so long. I knew this, I had almost busted myself so many times in Papua New Guinea when the customs officer became our friend. In retrospect, I think he was trying to impress me, but I don't think he realised how much his immigration officer status scared off us yachties. I bid him farewell and continued to follow the path laden with pigs and sheep and chickens and trash. I was just back at my launch post when I watched the water taxi pull up to drop off Tiaan and Selina and chug off towing the fishing boat they had rescued on the way. My heart raced as I swam back. I'd been anxiously praying all day. How were they? What did the doctor say?

My heart was heavy as I lugged myself aboard Papi. I knew already that they had lost the baby, I could feel it. We tried to celebrate life anyway, with a braai, as the lightning lashed out around us. We laughed and tried to keep each other high. I joined Tiaan and Selina for another shore excursion simply to find the internet. But it was a little too successful and I regretted messaging Karl. Oh well, I would do damage control next time. Tiaan and I sat on opposite sides of the cockpit ruminating life. His life had just massively changed again. Mine needed to. It was time to step up and reclaim my life, take control, and be the woman I was born to be.

21

Bahamas Baby

I*t was quite dramatic raising the anchor for what may well be the last leg of our trip together.* We bid farewell to the weird, wonderful, begging but beautiful island and set sail up the coast. We all had the same destination in our hearts, but the reality of it was uncertain. Tiaan and Selina had agreed to sail the vessel into the States, and they planned to follow through with their commitments. Only Tiaan had been denied a US visa when he had applied in South Africa. He had to try again in Nassau, in the Bahamas. Selina hadn't realised that in order to sail into US waters, an actual visa was necessary, not merely an ESTA, which she had used before. And I was literally in the same boat.

With all the plan changes and my jumping ship, I was too late for any of the potential jobs I had lined up in the Caribbean. Lynn and Todd had some excellent ideas of what I might do in or from the States. But obviously, I needed the visa too. And that's why we were headed straight for Nassau.

Our world was overwhelmingly beautiful. So much so that I had to nap. I took two morning naps, and another two in the middle of my workout session. The water kept changing colour as I lay face down on the trampoline watching the transformation beneath the boat. Lynn came out to join my non-stretch. We lay next to each other in silent awe. How lucky we were to have so much beauty in our lives.

The engine sputtered and died so many times that evening that we struggled to work out what was wrong, but we were simply caught in a fishing trap. We held lights as Tiaan dived in to free us. I'm glad I escaped bed for the occasion, the stars were putting on a light performance of note, dissolving into the distant red glow of mainland Haiti. The dolphins carried us past Jamaica. And a plethora of cruise ships passed as we sailed by Cuba with a new pod. Turks and Caicos glowed on our starboard side as we continued north through our daily routines. Writing, reading, workouts, laughing, fishing, cooking, feasting.

Even in the pitch blackness, I could make out the fog for it hazed the stars. The motor purred as we inched along at four-ish knots, manually correcting course as we chugged along past Grand Iguana Island. I'd been in the midst of yet another adventure dream when Selina came to knock. I thought I had lain still for long enough to memorise all the details, but two hours later, as I sat in the cockpit after a picturesque sunrise, it was all gone. All I had left were the remnants of coffee and a warm arm for, at seven a.m., the sun was already trying to cook me. The clouds reflected the surreal turquoise waters. As we sailed and motored the day kept growing in beauty.

We passed a few sailing boats and a fishing boat before we sailed into an anchorage on Long Island. A host of elegant sharks came over to greet us and welcome us to their waters. They seemed polite in a threatening kind of way. We were just about to go exploring when we changed plans again. Todd wanted to get all the Nassau business over and done with. We filled up with fuel and tried to get one beer at the bar. But the miserable, incompetent, lifeless bartender took so long serving the handful of other customers that we untied from the dock and sailed off without it. The sharks sang their farewells in our wake. Friendly or unfriendly, we never had the opportunity to be properly introduced.

I straddled the deck cleaning up all the lines we'd just freed. I was on the verge of tears, but I held them back, almost suffocating myself. I tried to drown them in the ocean by surfing off the stern. When that failed, I simply put my snorkel and mask on and lay with my head in the water watching the changing contours and life unfolding below instead of dealing with life above. I wished that I was a fish and I could stay down there forever. Instead, *Papillon* tried to force me back to the real world by shooting sporadic jets of water down my snorkel.

Back in the cockpit, we cracked open Selina's non-alcoholic beers and added vodka. The simple addition made the disgusting beverage palatable. It reminded me of the recipe of life: sometimes all you have to do is add a dash of hope. And with that, there were dolphins and *Papillon*'s heartbeat started again. Yes, we didn't know what we were sailing into, but there was some hope attached. The future was unwritten, but the present was too good to be missing out on. We made an immediate decision to anchor and enjoy the luminous waters that engulfed us. We dived in and lost ourselves in the blues.

There we sat contemplating conch. I'd found a giant one and swum it back, but we weren't quite sure what to do with it. How did we get to the meaty goodness? Selina and I were in stitches in the kitchen as we tried to boil the critter out. Later we had hammers and screwdrivers and the whole crew was completely hysterical in fits of laughter. The ceviche was served before the evening excitement; we had waterspouts forming on the horizon. A strangely uncomfortable phenomenon that held us in both awe and mild panic. We kept the awe, and the panic was eventually replaced by a beautiful night sky as we sailed into the Tongue of the Ocean. We were still riding a fierce ocean where the tiny waves were deceivingly powerful.

We had great wind and Nassau was only a brick's throw away. I lay on the roof watching the clouds transform from a cool sunglasses man into a cartoon otter. The transformation continued into two people ballroom dancing and leaning in for a kiss, to a foxy lady leaning in and giving me a thumbs up. God seemed to have put on an immaculate display just for me. I wondered what kind of epic He had in store for me. It was nice to be reminded how powerful His hands were and that I was laying in them. Some sort of worry still stained the air, but we tried our best to suffocate it with joy.

UNEMPLOYMENT LOOKS BETTER WITH A TAN

The city lights shone freakishly bright as we chugged our way towards the capital. Five days out of Haiti, we found ourselves on another planet as luxury vessels and power boats intersected our path in the rising sun. We passed a cruise ship bigger than some countries and eventually came in to anchor. We tidied up while Lynn and Tiaan ventured ashore to clear us in. They quickly returned because we had to be docked to check in. I took the dinghy ashore to help secure lines. I was happy to be there because the captain was in a sour mood.

Customs took one look and decided that they did not need to step aboard. And while the majority of the crew went to immigration, Selina cooked, and I settled into the last pages of my book while rays leapt out of the water as I had only ever seen in Panamanian waters. Breakfast came just after one p.m. and we were all a little on edge. There was so much to do, but nobody had the motivation or the energy. The beer was too expensive, so we drank rum. We slowly got everything sorted before we escaped the boat's confines to find dinner at The Green Parrot.

The following day was even more strenuous seeing that nobody had slept. We were all overly anxious about Embassy Day. I was a nervous wreck pacing back and forward waiting for Tiaan and Selina to be ready. We were meant to be there at dawn but it was almost ten a.m. by the time we eventually set off. We had tried to do all the paperwork online the previous day, but the first appointments were weeks away. We needed to explain to them why we needed urgent appointments. I'm just glad that we walked! The streets were quiet and interesting until we passed the cruise dock where a tsunami of immaculately dressed tourists slowly flooded our path. We found the embassy at last with sweat burrowing down our faces, and hearts racing like the drums do, just before a sacrifice. We were met with a wall. There was no way in unless we had appointments. We had to pay first, even if we wouldn't be able to make our allocated time. We might be able to have them expedited, but that wasn't up to us.

Lynn and Todd agreed to wait another day and we moved *Papillon* back to the anchorage. We three sat in the marina abusing the Wi-Fi trying to complete the plethora of paperwork needed for the application for the umpteenth time. The Americans don't make it easy to get in! All done, I held my bank card in my hand and prayed over it. I didn't think I had enough funds to pay the application, but there was no other way I'd be sailing into America. $180 is a lot of money, and even more when you don't have any!

It worked. And the friendly Swiss reception lady was even nice enough to print my DS160 for me. She was just handing it back when a call came through on the radio. We missed the first one, but the "*Papillon*" part came through loud and clear. The second time we all heard it: a rouge boat was floating down the river and heading straight for *Papi*. Tiaan and Lynn (who had just arrived) were in the dinghy before the message ended. Selina and I turned our attention to prayer.

I'd imagined a sailing boat heading for them. But this was a rugged, unmanned, steel cargo ship floating downstream and headed straight at Todd. It took out another vessel first. Todd didn't have time to up-anchor but managed to fight it off with fenders. All we suffered was surface damage. The rescue party arrived a little too late, but fortunately, there were pictures to show and extra hands to re-anchor after the police ordered us to move.

Selina and I had managed to get visa appointments for the following morning. But Tiaan, who had already failed the application, was not as lucky. For him, expediting was not an option and he had to wait another two weeks. I returned home both broken and hopeful.

We re-anchored again to be closer to Eric Clapton, but his anchor was up before ours was down. We took another shore excursion to sort out insurance claims and to get visa photographs. While we failed on all accounts, it was happy hour and we did succeed in having a beer. But the crew was a wild sea of raging emotions. Nobody knew what would happen next.

The whole family went to the embassy together. We got ID pictures on the way and were segmented into the queue. Me near the front for the 9:15 a.m. appointment and Selina was near the back for 9:30. Tiaan sat on the sidewalk because he didn't even have an appointment. The citizens, Lynn and Todd, cruised straight in to fight his case. The line slowly crept inside as people were constantly being sandwiched in front and behind me. I was four people from the front when a familiar-faced checkered shirt turned around and said, "Adeena?" I smiled and greeted him with a hug wondering where I knew him from. I didn't have time to ask, he was sent straight in.

Security scan. Fingerprints. I carefully contemplated all the people around me, all of them nervous. All of them had their own reasons and stories for why they were there. We danced through rows and questionnaires. Familiar face and his partner slid in just behind me.

"The Mongol Rally?" I asked with some hesitation.

And I was right. Dan and his wife, Anita, were on honeymoon visa runs. They now lived in New York. I'd met him in Mongolia nine years earlier, and again in China and in Thailand the following year. How small the world was. They were the perfect distraction from all the stress floating through the crowds that surrounded us.

I endured a friendly round of interviews and moved to the second window for more interrogation. Another smile met me at the third window.

"How long will you be staying for?"

"Do you have any dependents?"

"What is your role on the boat?"

I handed her letters from Lynn and Todd and other people who had invited me to the States including Captain Kirk and James from *Fiddler*. She smiled and said that she had to check something. She returned at last and handed me a form

"I have decided to deny your visa."

I stared blankly at her and asked her, "Why?"

There had to be some sort of mistake.

"All the information is on that form."

She had handed me the generic denial form. There was no questioning. No reconsidering. No arguing. Just, "No." I smiled as I walked back outside. I didn't know what else to do.

22

And then they said No

E*veryone was as surprised as I was.* I tried to turn off all the emotions as Dan and I caught up on the years that had passed while we waited for Selina. Her visa had been approved.

We bid Dan and his wife farewell and I agreed to meet them at the Green Parrot later. While the others tried to sort out insurance matters, I crept into the bathroom at the cruise ship terminal and cried. I shook and wept and fetaled up on the floor in pain. I didn't care how dirty it was. Turning off the tears turned on some numbness that would not allow me to do anything. I exited the bathroom and sat statued between the hair braiders in blank.

Todd took his turn to fetal position a little later, while the rest of us went internetting to try and work our lives out. I had quite literally just made mine a living hell. Now that I had been denied an American visa, I was unlikely ever to get an ESTA either. Everything would have to be done via the embassy with a $180 fee attached to it. My rejection letter informed me that I could appeal in a second interview, but I would have to start the process all over again, including the payment. I didn't have the money. Also, I am a firm believer that everything happens for a reason!

The only person online was Karl. He reminded me that the internet wasn't going to solve any of my problems. So, I went to the Green Parrot to find friends instead. They weren't there yet, so I bought a happy hour bucket and made myself comfortable.

"Steve," introduced the man next to me, shaking my hand with a firm grip and a kind smile.

He asked for my story and shared his. He used to be an immigration officer and told me it was a 100% subjective decision whether people were denied or approved. He would have let me in. Now, he was a prison warden instead. He felt like he could make more of a difference there rather than simply breaking hearts with rejections. His friend was a lawyer, they were both very envious of my gypsy life! Dan and Anita still hadn't arrived, so I finished my beers and was just in time for Todd to pick me up for dinner. Roast chicken! This time it was Lynn's turn to break into tears. Tiaan took his turn later that evening.

When Lynn and I did a morning internet run, I discovered that there was more than one Green Parrot. Dan and Anita had been drinking by themselves, too. I touched base with home and scanned crewing websites for boating opportunities. The only person I really wanted to speak to was Jeandré. For some reason, my little big brother always happened to know exactly what to do.

Lynn and Todd decided to keep us all for as long as possible, so we set off towards the States. We would have a couple more days together and we would make the most of it before our family was torn apart by bureaucracy!

The sea was rough and I was sick with emotions and a belly that wanted to fight. But we had only a short sail over to Whale Cay and the dolphins swarmed over to welcome us in.

A thatch shelter with two deck chairs and half an umbrella were the only things that suggested that humans had touched the paradise beach. I ventured further inland and found stairs that led to a dirt road. I pondered all the tracks it had marking it. Snakes? Bicycles? And then I found the lizards and the skinks… man were they cute! I came across a ruin and realised that I was less afraid than I should have been climbing onto its roof. When your life is empty, you have nothing to lose. But my hands were full. As I met the family on the beach, I'd collected so many shells that I had to get creative with transporting them back home. Or at least the closest thing I had to a home; the floating castle that had given me family and purpose and restored my life. My home was about to be taken away from me.

"The first step in the journey is to lose your way."

– Galway Kinnell

Chubb Cay gave us an anchorage full of sunken treasures and conch. It also gave us the perfect sunset to crack open the rum and enjoy the wild beauty that engulfed us. It was a bad night sleeping and a terrible morning. The runs, the start of my period, and yet another broken toilet. And by 6:54 a.m. we had raised the anchor and were on our way to Bimini, the last stop for our floating family. I did not have a clue what would happen next and I needed to cry and scream and shit and I was hyperventilating. What would Tiaan and Selina and I find in Bimini? *God! We need a miracle.*

At least Todd's rice pancakes were fantastic. I tried to absorb the deliciousness of life aboard while I still had it. What a therapeutic journey it had been. A journey of love and acceptance. And learning that it is okay to make mistakes. A journey of letting people love me for the crazy person that I am while affording them the same courtesy. How beautiful life is when you stop fighting and enjoy the flow; the currents, the storms, and the calms.

The crew packed up their belongings as we motored the windless passage. And we finally caught a fish. I had thought how nice it would be to do the last workout aboard, but the mammoth knots in my shoulders wouldn't let me. So instead, I spent some quality time with my people and prayed my laundry dry.

I had a magical night's sleep trusting that it all really would be okay. I was on an adventure with God after all and He always had the best ideas and surprises hidden up His majestic sleeves. We awoke with the anchor being dropped at 01:04 a.m. After hugs and smiles, we all nodded off to bed. The others checked in on me just after nine a.m. because they had never seen me sleep that much and were slightly worried that I was dead. Quite the contrary really, I felt more alive than I had in a long time! Did I really just need sleep? Could it be that simple?

The blues. The beauties. The Bahamas. A divine landscape for raging emotions. We raised the anchor and continued our voyage around Bimini as the teeming rays fled from our path. We chugged past mega yachts and fishing boats and finally headed in towards Big Game Marina. Because that's what life was. The highlight of arrival was Tiaan tossing lines ashore and missing twice. The second time it went straight up and down and hit him on the head.

"Know any boats heading for Europe?" I asked our new friend after he had secured our lines.

"I guess you're just going to have to stay in Bimini forever," he replied with a wink.

"Maybe today really is my lucky day," I replied laughing.

"It's some poor bugger's lucky day for sure," he said. "They found him floating twenty miles offshore after he fell overboard."

Lynn and Todd checked us in and cleared themselves out of the Bahamas. Tiaan and Selina wandered off to find accommodation and I sat down with the Wi-Fi. I was going to do everything I could, even if my chances were less than dismal. I applied for an ESTA visa. If a miracle happened, I could always take the ferry or a plane and catch up! I drank a beer with my favourite boat people and hugged Lynn for luck before I ventured down the dock to solve my impending homelessness. They were setting sail out of the Bahamas at nine p.m. and we didn't have much time to make our other plans.

I started with the mega yacht that had waved at us on arrival, but there didn't seem to be anyone home, so I kept walking. I could see sailing masts in the next marina, so I headed towards them; it was worth a chance. The first boat had been torn apart for repair work, but they invited me for a BBQ if I was still around the following day. Even though I hadn't solved a single problem, I left with hope and a massive smile. Which is why the geriatrics at the pool started talking to me.

"Any of you going any place interesting?" I asked nervously, "like Europe perhaps?"

Laughter erupted and then stopped.

"Actually, the boat next to me is headed for France and they are looking for crew. But they are leaving tonight."

I stared at her wondering if she was joking because that sounded a little too impossible to be true.

"Are you being serious?"

"Thank you so much for interrupting our conversation about diesel engines," she said as I followed her down the dock, "I'm old, I was worried that might be the last conversation I ever had. You were the most exciting thing that happened to any of us all day."

Eight marinas down, I found a vacant ketch. I hugged my guardian angel goodbye and sat down to wait. I was almost comfortable when a young French-speaking man came out of the showers.

"Hi!" I said, jumping to my feet, "I hear you are looking for crew."

"Yes, we were, but we have just confirmed our crew. A girl will meet us in Bermuda."

"Well, how about I join you as far as Bermuda?" I asked.

"You'll have to take that up with the captain. But, do you want to see the boat?"

"Adeena," I said, following him aboard.

"Gil," he replied.

Gildas, the captain, arrived while I was sipping a cup of water on the 46-foot Amel.

"Is it just you?" asked the captain trying to decide if this was a good idea.

"Yes," I replied and paused, "And my teddy bear."

"Is it a big bear?" Asked Gildas, smiling.

"It's a very big bear."

They both burst out laughing. It was agreed that I would move aboard after dinner, they'd be setting sail around midnight, at high tide.

I found Tiaan and Selina on the way back. They had a few options, but nothing they were too excited about. We walked home together and found Lynn cooking and Todd on the BBQ. We were in for a meat feast! Such different people we all were, but what a perfect mix of crew.

It was a good thing I disturbed the new neighbour by asking him to take pictures of us because he just happened to be heading back to Nassau slowly and wanted company. Tiaan and Selina moved aboard while I lugged my belongings to the dock. At nine p.m. sharp, after rounds of hugs and many tears, we cast *Papillon* off and watched her sail off without us.

87 days.

8120.2 miles.

The end of one beautiful life chapter and the start of the next.

23

Big Bear

Tiaan and Selina helped me carry my belongings across to the marina and my old crew was traded for a new one.

"What's the name of the boat?" Tiaan turned around to ask, as an afterthought, so that he could track us.

"Grande Ourse," said my new captain. "It means Big Bear."

All the earlier laughter suddenly made sense. Some things in life are just meant to be!

The third crew member's flight had been cancelled, so the new plan was to sail over to Freeport to pick him up. There would be some problems with me not being able to speak French, but we would work that out in time. Maybe it was time for me to learn? Was it by chance I'd been to French Guiana and Martinique and Haiti on a French-named boat, before hopping aboard with the Frenchies?

It was a smooth transition from helm to helm, and I took the first watch with confidence. By one a.m., the following day, we'd arrived and scouted Grand Bahama for a place to secure ourselves till dawn. It was an odd mind shift into another world. One paved with mega yachts and vacation makers.

It took a while, but we found our new crew member in due time. Leandre had just cycled from Chile to Brazil and was on his way home to France. We loaded him and his bicycle up and went to glean supplies for our crossing. I had an internal freak out when I watched Gildas throwing groceries into the trolley without checking prices. I'd seen how much a few measly items had cost Lynn and Todd. I knew I had very little money left. Luckily Leandre was on the same page because he ventured into the back office to ask if anything was expiring. And that's how we ended up with a trolley full of 70% reduced deliciousness. We taxied home and cooked up a feast before discovering that it was our new skipper's birthday. We took the opportunity to disturb all the neighbours with our singing for him before casting off.

Food preparations and preservations continued as we sailed into the Atlantic with our captain at the helm. It didn't take long for Leandre to get sick, but it didn't kill his spirit. The crew remained full of life and energy and laughter. We took two-hour watches seeing as there was no autohelm. With almost no wind, two hours felt like it dragged on forever. Eventually, my turn to sleep came and I dropped down both happy and exhausted.

Every glorious day should begin with coffee. And seeing as we still had bananas to salvage, I added banana bread to the equation. We caught our first fish, but it was too big, so we threw it back and caught another two before lunch. Partly because of the baking, and partly because I was foreign, but mostly because the Frenchies couldn't remember my name, I was called "Farine," which in Spanish is "Harina" which is close to "Adeena." Or so they said.

The rest of the day was spent reading, writing, drawing and laughing. As the setting sun finally dimmed, a "Happy birthday" balloon drifted past scoring even more laughs.

Three days later, after much laughter, chilling, sunset workouts, and good food; the wind died. The motor saved us for a while, but it didn't take long to realise that we had no oil. The five-day sail, as was originally planned, was more than optimistic. *Grande Ourse* had a new crew member meant to be joining the ranks the following day. The captain decided to radio a nearby tanker to get a message through to Sophie. We called another to get weather information too. We needed to find the wind. We were informed that we were going the wrong way. It's a hard job explaining to motor vessels that you are steering in the wrong direction to find the right wind. As the captain so aptly put it, "We were prisoners of the wind."

It was strange being on a couple-free boat. And, as we got to know each other better, we found that we all had our own share of heartaches, throbs and each of us had our question marks. The captain had his girlfriend and the rest of us held those big question marks close to our hearts. Those people we had let go of (physically at least), but who still seemed to make our hearts race. The mere thought of them kept us warm on cold nights. Not that there were many of those in the Caribbean.

Something else was happening to me, something new. Onboard we played a little game of magical beds. Depending on the tack and where the captain crawled up (he was not a man of habits), we would each take our turns to claim a bed for the night. Sometimes I would end up a little too close to other crew members. While I was trying to fall asleep, my libido was starting to wake up. There were nights when I wouldn't be able to sleep, my heart thumped too loud. The ocean had birthed some wild creatures within me. To deal with it, I added an extra workout regime to my days.

Slowly we advanced towards Bermuda, but the wind would bounce between nothing and 17 knots, which was barely a whisper. We sent a few more messages via freight ships through to Sophie, when we could. We made the most of the hot windless days and the company. The stars were plentiful by night, and every so often phosphorescent dolphins would streak magic around the vessel.

Sophie… If she gives up waiting for us, could I steal her place?

I wished upon a shooting star for God to paint my perfect path.

I woke up with the VHF radio. I thought that it was mere routine communication, but the captain had accidentally pressed the distress button.

"A-dee-naaah," he said, seeing me stir. "I would like to uh

orchestrate an uh oil de-liv-er-eey with the uh vessel nearby."

I wiped the sleep from my cheek and eyes and tried to drown my husky morning voice with water. The dawn light was beautiful, even if my eyes were still adjusting to it. I breathed in the beautiful sunrise and followed the captain's orders.

"*Akoya, Akoya, Akoya.* This is Sailing Vessel *Grande Ourse*."

I really needed to learn how to pronounce the name of our vessel! We exchanged coordinates and they laughed when I said we were making 2.5 knots. Compared to the previous day, we were flying! They laughed even more when I told them the minute quantity of oil we required. The vessel came into view while I stole the captain's coffee. Excitement built as the vessel turned on a collision course. It played out perfectly as they delivered the oil by a rope off the stern. The captain turned us in while Leandre climbed down to catch it and hand it to me. Such a simple delivery gave us both a future and a hope. I radioed through some heartfelt gratitude and had just returned to the cockpit when the cry came: "Bollen[33]!" A majestic orca came up to say hi and dived down underneath us. It disappeared as magically as it had arrived and when we were sure it was well and truly gone, we turned our focus to important issues and rehydrated our engine. It wasn't even seven a.m. and already the day was rich with awesome (and slightly fermented pineapple). Seeing as we once more had a functional engine, the wind returned.

I had an angry sleep. I don't even know what exactly that is. Or why I had it, but it was angry alright! I was in terrible form as I climbed my way to take the morning shift. But by Jove, the world was beautiful! I took the helm and wiped the sleep from my eyes. As the kettle boiled, I eased into a fresh start. It was just me and God on the quietest morning ever. We needed to talk. I had so much to be thankful for and I needed to commit my future to him once more.

The Lord directs our steps, so why should we try and understand everything along the way?
– Proverbs 20:24

---

[33] "Whale."

Life is a simple journey when you take it one step at a time. And it is full of surprises. Our day was filled with hundreds of dolphins frolicking in our bow wake. The whole crew was now in the habit of joining workout sessions and the playlists that we danced and trained to were extraordinary! They attracted birds and fish and our dinner was delicious!

Sailing jellyfish lined our path on day nine as we sipped on our morning coffee. We were only 137 miles out and my mind raced. What would Bermuda throw at me? A job? Another boat? Bankruptcy? Would Sophie still be there? Would my ESTA application be approved? Where would I sleep? What would I eat? Who would I meet? *Okay, breathe Adeena! That's tomorrow's problem and tomorrow will look after itself.* By nightfall, the wind had shifted and we could see the glow of the island. Only 54 miles remained until the determining of my fate!

UNEMPLOYMENT LOOKS BETTER WITH A TAN

24

Ocean Blues and Baguettes

S*unrise and the spinnaker.* Before I had a chance to get coffee, I was on the VHF to Bermuda radio. What was our call sign? Registration? MMSI? EPIRB number? Life raft manufacturer? Satellite phone number? SSB? My captain was cursing the English. There were 20 minutes left on my watch and 13.9 miles to the anchorage. It was official, I was shitting myself.

Dozens of boats raced out of Bermuda as we entered. 15- 20 – maybe even 40. I sat with a cup of rooibos tea wondering if one of those was meant to be my exit ticket, but I stopped myself.

You're always where you are meant to be!

Swiss boats, German boats, Swedish boats….

Breathe Adeena, breathe.

Leandre came and joined me on the bow, he could read my thoughts. He threw a brotherly hug around me and assured me it would all be okay.

"I'm going to miss you, Farine. I wish you were coming with us. Maybe Sophie isn't here."

We circled the anchorage for over an hour waiting for dock space to clear in. It was anything but a friendly welcome, but we had made it. Leandre jumped off to find a good place to park his bike, and Gildas left in order to find Wi-Fi to contact Sophie. While Gil tidied everything up, I chatted to a Canadian who had just booked a flight because he had given up trying to find a boat to get him home. I wondered if I would end up in the same ~~boat~~ plane.

Sophie actually existed! And she was still there and patiently awaiting them. Despite not receiving any of the plethora of messages we had tried to send through to her, she understood that sailing trips rarely run to schedule. I let the rest of the crew get a head-start on beer while I made crewing posters to decorate the town with. It was a pretty place and I enjoyed exploring it.

It still wasn't happy hour when I caught up so I busied myself a little longer. I was so excited to finally receive my beer that I knocked the whole table's over with enthusiasm. An expensive mistake I couldn't really afford. But when you're looking brokeness in the eye, I tend to make it blink first!

Leandre and I ventured off to explore the beautiful island and in the light of the setting sun, it was perfect! Gildas was finally tying up to collect us when I discovered that the man I had casually been chatting to on the dock was looking for crew. I jumped into his dinghy to find out more. And, while I had mixed feelings about him, I wasn't going to miss an opportunity. I greeted Gildas and took off with my new friend to see his boat.

After the tour of his boat and a chat, I accompanied him to a BBQ on another vessel. You know you are throwing a decent party when there are so many people aboard that your boat begins to sink. It was an entertaining evening that restored my hope. By the end of the night, I had multiple options and plenty of intoxication.

"Please can we have our Princess back?"

Gildas had rowed over to collect me and I stumbled back aboard *Grande Ourse* grinning wok-eyed.

I climbed into the cockpit to watch the sun rise over the beautiful island. What a magical place! It was only when I returned inside that I found Teddy "buen". He now had balls, a cigarette and alcohol in hand. One night with the boys and he had been utterly corrupted!

Four missed calls from Rupert. Once connected to the Wi-Fi, there were always some surprises. He was heading to Bermuda in ten days or two weeks and he needed crew. One Facebook post really can go a long way! The lively Englishman had brightened up the woes of our Engine problems in Panama years before. We'd kept in contact and caught up for laughs a half handful of times since. He had a lot to teach and I craved both adventure and growth. It was perfect. If I could find a temporary home before then, that is.

I ventured into the pub that I had been stealing internet from and there stood a mob of hungover sailors that I had met the night before. My new Danish friend, David, offered to check with the owner of his vessel if I was allowed to take up residency on S/V *Amazing Grace*. It all sounded a bit too amazing to be true, but when you're on an adventure with God, it always is.

My phone beeped again.

"Are you still looking for a boat?"

Because nothing in my life was confirmed yet, I agreed to meet another captain at five p.m. I took a walk. I bought a scone and a ginger beer and the cashier sang as she cashed up. A friendly local directed me to a nice spleening[34] spot and I found a shady tree to perch under and enjoy my feast. The world was beautiful, but money woes were consuming me. What did I have left in the world? $20 US and R1600[35]?

I'm going for broke. I know I shouldn't worry because it always works out okay. YOU WILL ALWAYS HAVE ENOUGH!

---

[34] The word I have adopted for soul-searching, thinking, processing thoughts and ruminating life.

[35] Approximately $83 US at the time.

There only seemed to be two leagues of sailors in Bermuda: Scandinavians and French. The Scandinavians found me waiting and gave me the great news that I was welcome aboard *Amazing Grace*. And then a smiling French face headed in my direction and I knew it was him immediately.

"Adeena?"

I guess there weren't that many females around, especially not ones lugging around waterproof bags.

"Clemont," he said, smiling too widely.

A bearded man headed over too, "Guy".

I listened half-heartedly to the proposition they were giving me. I knew I had a ride and I knew that I had a home so I already knew I would be turning them down. But did I want to see the boat? Of course.

I hopped into Guy's (pronounced "Geee" of course, he was French) tender and we sped over to *Turia*, a picturesque Amel 55. It was perfect. Too perfect. White and teak and not even four years old. My Gypsy soul quivered. I told them I had another offer, but said I would think it over and we agreed to meet the following day at ten a.m. to make the said decision.

Clemont drove me back and I thought we were headed for sundowners with the token Englishman, as was previously discussed. But he had other plans.

"I need help with my ESTA," he said.

The simple word still stung me, but I was feeling generous, so I agreed. I also suspected that he had some other plans, nobody needs help with an ESTA. The 41-year-old was all alone in the world. He was born in French Guiana, grew up in Panama and Columbia and had both his parents die at an early age. He did a bunch of random jobs and proceeded to become a pilot and then a sailor, in ten-year work cycles. He had spent years getting his boat ready to sail, spending a fortune in preparations to take her around the world. When he was finally ready to go, he sailed her for a day and a half and hit a tanker, bringing his dream to a very abrupt end. He was a beautiful soul, but he seemed to enjoy dwelling on the hardships of life! We entered the bar and bumped into Leandre. I have still never met such a kindred soul! Cycling, sailing, hitch-hiking... I don't believe in star signs, but his birthday is only one day after mine, so maybe there really is something to it? We were distracted by more sailors but finally made it to the bar to order. Clemont continued talking and I continued listening, still vaguely distracted by the Leandre in the corner. Was he jealous? Did I want him to be?

Clemont was tired of hardships in life and now he wanted a home and a family. He needed security. He was flying back to France to finally start his life. He didn't want to leave until he knew that Guy had good crew. Clemont had been paid to deliver the boat from Martinique, but they'd had very little wind, so a third of the way across the Atlantic he had ordered the boat to turn around and head back. He had claimed that he simply needed to refuel. In reality, he had wanted to leap off the boat and speed up starting his life. He knew he was letting Guy down. He was going to use the little he had to build a future. I thought about telling him that he would always have enough, but I still couldn't get a word in.

The sales pitch to me turned from crewing with Guy to his wife-hunting. While he was a beautiful man with a similar spirit, he had no roots and needed to find some before he could grow into someone ready for a relationship. I watched *Grande Ourse* getting themselves ready to leave and I tried to wrap up the conversation.

"Bonne nuit," I said casually, "I'll see you tomorrow."

He wasn't finished talking, but I knew I had heard enough. He needed to find his own path.

I was delighted to be home with my Frenchies. We cooked up a feast together and then we cracked open Sophie's rum. They were such a wild group that I was sad I wouldn't be crossing the Atlantic with them. We laughed late into the night and I was the first to crawl into bed, I needed it.

Grande Ourse went into the dock to take on fuel and while they did their chores, I ran off to try and speak to family. My verse for the day was Matthew 6:25:

" *[25] Therefore I tell you, do not worry about your life, what you will eat or drink; or about your body, what you will wear. Is not life more than food, and the body more than clothes? [26] Look at the birds of the air; they do not sow or reap or store away in barns, and yet your heavenly Father feeds them. Are you not much more valuable than they?"*

And while speaking to Mom, I knew exactly what I needed to do.

UNEMPLOYMENT LOOKS BETTER WITH A TAN

Jeandré simply laughed. And when Guy arrived early, I cut the conversation short. I gulped as I cleared my throat to say, "No."

25

Fixing Engines with Positivity

I'd made the wrong decision. *When will I learn?* I couldn't sleep, I was beating myself up so badly. Instead, I lay praying that some other crew would miraculously appear to replace me. I'd started to say "no", but Guy's eyes had pleaded and his beautiful soul cried out to mine for help. All he wanted to do was get home to his wife, and he needed help. How could I say no to that?

The French man spoke virtually no English, and apart from the essentials ("Baguette, pain au chocolat, crêpe, santé…"), I had no French. We walked around town stripping down all the posters that we had respectively put up. We had similar tastes in community notice boards. Clemont had packed up his 90 kg of gear and moved ashore so that I could take his cabin aboard. He had now washed his hands clean of the mission by gifting it to me.

There were a few things that needed doing, and Guy humoured me by allowing us to hitchhike to Hamilton, the capital, to carry them out. I could tell that he was loving it. We handed in the satellite phone to get repaired and busied ourselves exploring the forts and the supermarkets. Guy was impressed that I could procure so much free fresh produce and started challenging me to get more. We still hadn't discussed costs and I was nervous to raise the topic, but Guy made it clear that I was helping him, so he would help me. My luck got even better as we found the Salvation Army and I walked out with a large pile of English books that cost me a whopping 0.50c for the lot.

Because there were delays with the phone, there was time to sort out other concerns, too. While Guy continued his quest, I found stray Wi-Fi in a park and got my other matters in order. With all my life woes sorted, a plethora of low-cost and free groceries, and a fixed satellite phone, we hitchhiked back just in time for our guests. Guy thought he had only invited one boat, but three arrived. All from luxury Amels, all French, all headed in the same direction as us. I was amidst a new league of sailors.

I had just finished connecting bird-scaring-fishing-wire[36] to our mast when *Grande Ourse* arrived to throw Teddy back. They had just returned from their circumnavigation of the island and were doing final preparations to sail on, across the Atlantic. I hugged them goodbye and was sad I wouldn't be seeing them again anytime soon. Gildas agreed we could keep the friendship if I won the lottery and bought his boat from him. Gilles promised to come sailing with me as soon as I had my own boat. In return, I promised to visit the brewery he was planning on starting up in Belgium. Leandre and I had plans to cycle the west coast of Africa the following year, so it wasn't a real goodbye, it was more like a "see you later."

I was merrily downloading music and audiobooks ashore when Leandre found me again. The hug was needed, but so was I. They weren't allowed to leave without taking me off the crew list. I followed them to immigration. But I had to find Guy too, I wasn't allowed off the one crew list without joining another. Eventually, I hugged them all again, took their trash, untied their lines and waved them off across the Atlantic, hoping to catch them in the Azores.

---

[36] Our deck was nicely decorated in various berry-coloured poops and I was already tired of cleaning the artworks off.

"What's wrong?" asked my local friend Phoopa as I sat aloof on the dock.

Before I knew it, I was aboard his glass-bottomed boat and off on a fishing adventure around the island.

"Sunday sessions are the best," he said, offering me a beer.

After more beer, wine, snorkels, and much laughter, we picked up his grandkids and I hitched home. I was still on my way when Guy passed in the dinghy and I jumped boats. The timings were all perfect.

My reputation preceded me, and all the local stores now had expiring goods ready for me. Only it was too much. I became the gifter of asparagus and other yummy things to a good portion of the world's sailing community before we were finally ready to leave. A few last checks, many final hugs, and by six a.m. I was still awake with my mind racing. It was a beautiful day, but it was a big one!

After breakfast, we raised the anchor and started towards customs. There were no lines to be found and we needed them to dock. Try as I might I couldn't get it across to my skipper that there was no way we could tie up without them because he had no idea what I was talking about. Perhaps the journey would be more challenging than I imagined. The fuel dock held even more miscommunications, but we eventually had everything we needed, including banana bread and new friends. I snaked down to lick the land goodbye and before we knew it, we were veering out of the Saint George's Channel and into the Atlantic. Me and Guy on *Turia* and two other French boats heading in the same direction. I called Bermuda radio to announce our departure. I forgot the phonetic "A" as I spoke. Nobody ever forgets "Alpha."

I was home, again, in the ocean. But the wind was nowhere to be found. The day disappeared to the soundtrack of the engine as we tried to keep up with Sailing Vessels *Muskali* and *Anthea*. We feasted on portobello mushrooms and asparagus as the sun put on a setting performance to bless our voyage. And, after a short night, it rose again with similar splendour.

I was busy helping Guy raise the ginormous spinnaker pole when I saw it, a rip in the genoa. The aluminium furler had torn right through. While Guy radioed an Amel specialist on one of the other boats, I set about finding duct tape and cable ties. But his solution taught me that a butter knife and dishcloth are sometimes just as useful. It worked, but I had a sullen captain who was as uncertain about the journey ahead as I was. Had I made the right decision? I knew he was asking himself the same questions! Anyway, it was too late to change anything by then. I just wondered if there was a way to bring joy – real joy – to the vessel. God knew where we were at.

I was exhausted when I lugged myself into the cockpit on the third day. There were 33 knots of wind and the rain was pouring, but the captain was smiling. Despite the foreboding weather, I liked that start to the day! I started to get braver aboard the electronic vessel and experimented with the plethora of dials and buttons. Then I accidentally turned the boat straight back to Bermuda. I worried for a minute but quickly learned that all mistakes could be rectified and set us back on course. Mistakes remind you that you are human. Mistakes teach you.

And then the wind died. But so had the engine, it wouldn't start. There's plenty of room for problems on a boat when everything is electronic, including the keys. I made a few suggestions, but Guy was already on the radio with the other boats. In a panic, he began tearing the boat apart looking for a solution. I had seen too many problems in the past and knew that he should simply have sat down and had breakfast first. But he didn't understand that yet. When you haven't experienced the power of "chill", you can't comprehend it. I helped him get to the fuses and the battery. No luck. We toyed with everything the others had suggested. And while Guy got them back through the airwaves, the rains started plummeting down. I covered up all the exposed electronics and said a silent prayer. I tried the key again and the engine roared to life.

"Adeena just fixed the engine with positivity," Guy said and the other boats roared with laughter.

That's a step better than the garlic I had used on a previous boat. I love being on adventures with God.

Poor Guy, all he wanted was simple food, but I would not let the vegetables rot, so we ate an abundance of them. Even my pee had changed colour from all the nutrition my body was receiving. Scurvy was as far away from our minds as the world was getting. We were quickly learning to communicate without language and enjoy our differences. Joy was on the rise and the days began to fly past in perfect rhythm with hard work, laughter, blues, dolphins, and much-needed naps.

The other boats veered north and we continued on our route towards the Southern Azores en route to Morocco. The blues were ours alone, shared only with dolphins and whales and fish, even if I couldn't get any on the hook.

It was four a.m. and, under the brilliance of the full moon, the chaos of the sea was frightening. I didn't want to think about all the things that could possibly go wrong out there. I was just glad that I didn't have to hand-steer it. I wondered how *Grande Ourse* was faring. Were they still happy and smiling and singing? Or had they passed the honeymoon phase? I wondered how Sophie was fitting in with the boys. Had she hooked up with one of them? I wondered if we were close. Or if we had already left them in our wake.

The sun was rising so perfectly that my whole body was awash with love. *I don't know where to look for it or how I will find it, but I need it.* I thought about Karl. *Has he moved on? Have I? Should I? Where do I meet my match? Does such a thing even exist? My life is epic! I will not add anyone to this who does not hold to that! There's Leandre – But he's simply a beautiful clone. Is that what I need?*

Actually, sitting out here in the middle of this fiery sea, there isn't even a point in thinking about it. I don't know where I will wash up, or when, but God knows what I need. And hopefully, by then, my heart will be beating fully again!

༆

My mind raced along with the boat. Guy was going to leave *Turia* in Morocco while he went home for wife time. But I knew Morocco was not my final destination, I needed to work. And having a European passport made Europe the logical choice.

Should I head for Spain or Portugal? Or would the Netherlands or Switzerland or Sweden make more sense so that I can make more money?

I had so many options that I didn't know where to begin.

One step at a time Adeena. God reminded me last night how many perfect [for me] unplanned, fun jobs He has lined my path with. From places that I had never dreamed of. I am excited to see how this pans out. I am also excited for eight a.m. to come, I can't wait to get some sleep!

Sleep was challenging in the wild waves and I had to wedge myself into my bunk and hold on. I woke up refreshed, but wondered how to make the captain's spirit soar. I don't think that he had ever been the over-joyous type, but the seasick version of him was a shadow. I tried to pray, but my never-resting brain kept interrupting. Why doesn't it have an off button?

It was a new month and while I decided to celebrate with coffee, the captain decided to celebrate by changing his insurance policy to a cheaper one that didn't cover cyclones. I had two waves hit me in the face while I balanced the ariel as high as I could so that he could get connectivity. I was grumpy. I needed coffee. I needed communication. I needed a hug. I needed to cry. Oh yes, PMS. A terrible excuse. But somehow a beautiful reality. What a relief it is when the blood stops boiling and starts flowing. We have to embrace the cycle, and let it flow.

With the captain's needs met, I sat in the pilot chair holding on for dear life as I rode the ocean-bull, trying to balance my coffee while spewing my emotions onto paper. I was tired of being in survival mode. Life was a never-ending array of basic needs being met and challenges being overcome. There were so many things that I wanted in life that I couldn't die yet. The sea was fierce, the wind was relentless. Drinking water levels were an ever-present concern. As was battery power seeing that we were on a very electronic vessel. I swore to myself that I needed to change something in my life. I wanted to enjoy it once again. I was tired of fighting simply to stay alive. I was ready to relish the simpler things without the stress the ocean threw at us. I was far from safe now, but I knew I would be there soon. Wherever I was heading, it was going to be a safe space! I was ready for it!

It was a Monday morning. I had only had three hours of sleep, but I felt completely alive! The four a.m. morning glow reminded me how beautiful life was. It also confirmed my suspicions that we were very much in the wrong time zone. The seas calmed and the captain decided to save vegetables of his own accord. So, while I worked out in the cockpit, the pressure cooker produced a feast of cauliflowered French cuisine. The sun set exquisitely and I was reminded again of how I will always have enough. I WILL ALWAYS HAVE ENOUGH. I should write it 1000 times and tattoo it on my being. I know it so well, but I am always forgetting it.

Sadly, calm and Zen were short-lived aboard *Turia*. And as I crawled out of bed and climbed the mountain-stairs to the cockpit, I already knew we were in for a tough day. Boats were trying to run us over and the rain absorbed the wind so it was a constant wet battle dancing with the sails. When we finally gave up and turned on the engine, I sat down to spleen and somehow get over my disappointment. It was suffocating me. We were skipping the Azores and heading straight for Morocco. The captain wanted his wife more than he wanted a break and an adventure. I was sad that I was missing the one thing I was most excited about, but I knew I was always where I needed to be.

What other lessons was I forgetting?

- *If you do all your "work" before you make time to do what you want to do, you will never end up doing what you want to do.*
- *Sometimes you just need to rip up your to-do list and sit back and chill.*
- *Don't ever settle for second or even third or even fifth best. Decide what you want and only settle for that.*
- *Perfect is boring. Make more mistakes!*
- *If you are being the best you that you can possibly be then you really are mastering life. Never try to be anyone else.*
- *I can make all the plans that I like, but God definitely has some better ones!*

All I wanted to do was stop disappointing God. And then I realised how wrong that idea was. God is not human; He does not get disappointed. He's like the ultimate dad and teacher. He gives us far more than simple stars for effort. He gives us abundance and we make Him proud! (Even when we do make mistakes.) I was suddenly even proud of myself. I felt worthy. I felt loveable. I felt like anything was possible again.

I realized how my lack of finances and plans had made me feel like a lower creed of human. But that was simply by society's standards and I didn't care much for those. Looking back, my heart and soul were so full, my bank balance shouldn't have mattered!

I celebrated my spleenings with an "appecable" (able to be pecked at) assortment of leftovers for lunch. And then I got back on my laptop and tried to write books and blogs. I was just getting comfortable and creative when Guy interrupted to let me know that there was something on my line. I squinted in the strange lighting. The sky below the random clouds was green. I'm sure I had never seen anything like that before or since. Both Guy and I were expecting the line to be coated in algae again like it had been the handful of times that I had bothered to throw it out. By the time my eyes had adjusted to the bizarre light, it looked more like cardboard. But my positivity had it transform into a fish by the time I had it on the deck. I reeled in a tuna!

Dinner was going to be great and I hoped that Guy would let us celebrate it with a beer. It was a beer kind of day: windless with the sun waking up to be in full force again. We had 650 miles to go. I washed the blood from the deck and Guy was already smiling in the companionway with beers in hand. And for dinner, he surprised me even more, he had chilled a bottle of wine. We got the real crockery out for the occasion.

The feast was delicious, but the smell of blood stained my hands through five tacks and two restless nights. It wasn't a bad thing though, I suddenly got excited because I knew how to finish my first book and still keep the same title: *First We Ate Your Wife*[37]. When I did finally find rest, there was a knock on the door. I thought I must have skipped my alarm, but I still had two hours. I closed my eyes. The knock came again. I expected a catastrophe. But someone was simply calling us on the VHF, or at least Guy thought they were.

---

[37] When floating adrift in the Pacific with Karl, we reeled in the second sizable dorado in as many days. It had been following us all day as if it had been searching for its missing partner. I had looked it in the eye and asked if it was the husband. It didn't reply of course, but it didn't need to – I knew! I also knew then what I wanted my book to be called.

"Sailing boat. Sailing boat. Sailing boat."

We changed to channel 06. Can you believe that they were English? And can you believe that I still remembered how to speak the language? Almost an hour disappeared in conversations in my native tongue until the boats were too far away to maintain contact.

I wandered into the cockpit to see what the world was like. Cloudy. Very cloudy. And the pigeon that had joined our crew the previous day was marching about like he was on duty. As he attempted his second test flight, I saw the fin and ran to the bow.

"Dolphin," I cried.

But judging by the size, it was more likely a whale that hovered just long enough to say a friendly "hello."

Talk about a bizarre morning. This was all before eight a.m. And all before coffee. For the first time in my life, I had a Frenchman make me French toast. Only they call it "Pan Perdu" which translates as "lost bread."

The boat was always awash with music and there was a recent air of joy that spanned even further than the airwaves. Guy's classical music fitted most occasions, but I know he appreciated my alternative playlists too. We were getting so close to land that he was excited. For me, the terror had started rising and I started chanting to the music just to remind myself "You will always have enough."

The closer we got, the more boats filled our horizon and the AIS[38]. So, watches became a lot more focused. I thought the six ships we had with us for dinner were a lot, but when I took over at one a.m., there were 16. The AIS alarm became the new soundtrack for our existence.

Marine life carried us all the way to the Portuguese coast. It looked as rugged and wild as our raging ocean did. It seemed to be calling to me, but we kept it to port and sailed on towards Spain. I couldn't decide if I

---

[38] The Automatic Identification System (AIS). It is a receiver that transmits your boat's identifier and receives the signal from others. This aids you in knowing where they are and how you are moving in relation to them. While not all boats are fitted with or utilising this device, it is very useful in helping to avoid collisions. It is also the bane of your existence when the distance alarm can't be deactivated and you are in busy shipping areas.

was nervous or excited. I had so many unfinished projects that I needed to complete in the Atlantic. And I did, almost. But, by the time we reached the straights of Gibraltar and her crazy currents and mad traffic, it didn't matter anymore. And that was it, the end of the Atlantic. Or, as the French call it, the end of our "Transat." Guy and I both smiled through the stress of the traffic and got spat out in the Mediterranean.

The wind picked up and the glass water turned wavy. We were in the shallows and had only 1.2 meters of depth below our keel. With 20 to 30 knots of wind, we were flying! We cracked open a beer and cheered. And when looking for something even more celebratory, I discovered the bunches of grapes I'd frozen. They were perfectly refreshing in the heat of the afternoon. I defrosted our last frozen passage meal from Bermuda and by nightfall it was official, we had absolutely no asparagus left aboard. That was some sort of miracle.

I shivered my way through the first night watch and awoke Guy at about 11 to help with the sails. The wind and waves were mounting in a crazy fashion. By midnight, I was spent and dropped to bed. 1:21 a.m. and I was sure that I had overslept and missed my alarm. I hadn't. But there was absolutely no way I could sleep through all the rocking. And definitely not with the VHF emergency alarm going off every 20 minutes.

"Pan Pan Pan…".

At four a.m. I was really relieved to relieve Guy.

And that's where I currently sit. Wrapped up in my sleeping bag steering us straight into a silver moon. Less than 50 miles remain, but I am too tired to be scared or nervous.

I put it all into God's hands. And the boat too, my eyes were so tired they could barely stay awake. I did fall asleep eventually, but a minute later I woke up with the Pan alarm.

I was relieved when Guy took over, but I had just made it to my cabin when he called after me again. They were calling us on the VHF. This time it was serious, a refugee boat that Search and Rescue had been tracking had recently disappeared in the waters that we were sailing through.

"Please keep a sharp lookout for an inflatable boat with about 50 people in it."

I couldn't imagine being in an inflatable boat in those icy cold wild waters. How desperate must those people be to find freedom? I crawled into bed and lay there praying.

The last miles were spent vigilantly watching the waters and enjoying the beauty of the little islands we passed. And then the fish traps began. So did the stress. I'm not sure if it would have been better or worse if we shared a common language. But the last minutes were anything but pleasant. We reached the dock, but the bow thrusters weren't working so I ran back to throw a smiling face our stern line and then I saw my folly. One line had tangled itself into the propeller. Luckily, I relied on higher powers more than technology and eventually, we were firmly secured to safety.

The police boarded and searched the boat and checked our passports. We then followed them to immigration where we were officially welcomed into Morocco with the confiscation of our satellite phone, they're illegal in the country.

There was nothing left to do but to drink. And free up the line that I had accidentally gotten wedged in the propeller. With a little bit of muscle and a lot of faith, it all came free and finally, I felt like we had arrived. Back in Africa, back on the other side of the Atlantic. Back to square one where I had absolutely no plans and no idea what I was doing. But for arrival day, I wasn't going to let that bother me. Instead, we met the neighbours in the quiet marina and marvelled at the ghost town. It was Ramadan and the few people that we did see were all exhausted and almost lifeless. I needed life. I need adventure. I needed to somehow make some money. Actually, there were a lot of things I needed right then, but I wasn't worried (Yet) because my new mantra was: "I will always have enough."

UNEMPLOYMENT LOOKS BETTER WITH A TAN

26

Warning Signs of Your Gypsy Demise

I*t's Friday!* *15 June 2018, 03:57 a.m. and my alarm is screaming at me to get up and leap into a new chapter. Today Guy takes a taxi, to take a plane, to take another plane, to get to France. To Albertville, to his wife, to home.*

And me? Well, I have absolutely no idea what is about to happen to me. I have no idea what today holds or where I will sleep tonight. But I'm on an adventure with God and I will let Him be the leader.

We cleaned and boarded her up before we both bid farewell to *Turia*. She was a marvellous vessel and had given me more luxury than I had allowed myself in over a decade. A short taxi ride later, it was a sad farewell to my skipper. I was back to gypsy living and bear lugging. I sat on the side of the road in a little town wondering if any cars would actually pass to get me closer to somewhere that felt good. It was a long wait and people were nice enough to come out from little tea shops and houses to bring me coffee and fruit. There were plenty of desperate suitors to fend off. And equally as many people came over just to marvel at my shoulders. I covered them up.

The people were exceptional, and the country was begging to be explored, but I knew I needed a job and I didn't think that Morocco could offer me what I was looking for. Also, after the freedom of the ocean, I didn't like to be fully covered up in the heat. Yes, I wanted to travel and explore, but even more than a job, I craved a home. Morocco just didn't quite feel like that.

I hopped through shared taxis. For anyone who doesn't believe that all things are possible, you simply have to see seven people and their luggage squashed into a little car to be assured of it. I sampled some street food and tried to absorb, with my eyes, the world that was flying past me. From Nador, I took a bus to the border. With the breeze and the space, it felt like pure luxury. And then a kid tried to rob me through the window and the bus driver chased him with a brick. My illusions of grandeur were shattered.

I had a little troop of pickpockets trailing behind me as I ventured into a tiny store to try and spend my last dirham on unhealthy snacks. I failed; a little dirham goes a very long way!

SPAIN

Melilla could not have been more different. I hitched a ride into the centre and perched in a pristine park to take in my surroundings. It was a beautiful city. Strange how a country divide could have such opposing sides. I began walking towards the water. I forgot how difficult it was to move when carrying all of my belongings. *Why was my backpack so heavy?*

There were boats in every direction so I felt dizzy just trying to decide where to start. All I needed was a boat to the other side of the Mediterranean Sea. The marina staff thought it was unlikely, but I knew that all things were possible, so I tried my luck anyway. A few meters later, I bumped into some Canadians that I had met in Saidia. We had a quick catch-up before they offered to keep my bags with them. Such a simple gesture completely changed my life.

I spoke to a plethora of boats, but none of them seemed to be heading across to mainland Europe any time soon. So, I went to a bar and ordered a beer to mull over my life options and celebrate another border crossing. I took out my travel diary to write and clear my head. That's when I noticed that the TV was on: The Soccer World Cup. Spain vs Portugal. I had a sudden wave of excitement and enthusiasm and awe. I was so joyous, that I felt like I might burst. My words from years long gone suddenly came spiralling back to me. Back in 2010, when I hated football[39], I had to heighten my interest levels. To endure all 64 games for my World Cup contract, I had sworn to flightlessly travel to whichever country won. It had taken eight years and I had just about forgotten my promise, but there I was, sitting in Spain, the very same country that had won the tournament. The fact that it was on the African side didn't matter to me, nor that it took four times as long as predicted to get there. What are eight years in the spectrum of a lifetime[40]?

What an epic journey!!!! I'm not sure how I have survived all of it but here I am. Sitting in Spain, sipping a beer. I'VE DONE IT!

I did one more scout through the plethora of boats and then cut my losses. I walked to the ferry terminal wondering how much it would cost. The queue was long. One man and woman were having a loud domestic dispute. Kids were running everywhere. Most of the tourists were smartly dressed and freshly attired. I didn't fit in. But I also didn't care. So many people walked away looking dejected. I walked away with a reasonably priced ferry ticket for just after midnight.

I ventured off to explore the little city. It was beautiful and hot. And there was much distraction, so my arrival time back at my bags was much later than anticipated. And when beer and dinner distraction was awaiting me too, I almost missed the boat.

It seemed that all the other passengers had opted for cabins, so I

---

[39] "Soccer", to all you US readers.

[40] Don't answer this, it's rhetorical :)

had most of the communal seating area to spread out in. If it wasn't for the hyperactive kids who kept accidentally running over me on their way to everywhere, it was perfect!

There was a long queue to exit the ferry and a longer queue at immigration, but I had nowhere to be, so it didn't worry me. I splurged and bought myself a real coffee so that I could sit down and use the Wi-Fi to make life plans. Also, I felt like my journey was officially over now that I was in Malaga, mainland Spain. The Portuguese waiter assured me that Spain was better than Portugal for work. I knew that I had some good friends in Majorca[41] and I knew that it was one of the sailing capitals of Europe. Slowly my plan grew into a realisation of what I had to do. It was boating season and if I could just make it to Palma, I knew I would be alright.

Spain is probably the worst country that I have ever hitchhiked in. The people are lovely, but not when they leave you desperately melting on the side of the road. I walked for miles and had nothing but insults thrown at me. An Argentinian drove me a few kilometres to get me out of the city centre and a few hours later another car stopped to take me a brick's-throw further, but in the wrong direction. Before I knew it, I was even further away than when I had started. After the next ride, I was almost in tears and people could probably sense it because nobody even slowed down to say "hi". Not even out of curiosity. After a few hours of nothing, I decided that I needed beer.

I found both beer and English at the same time. And with the mention of a cheap hostel, I decided to follow the other beer purchaser in its direction. I negotiated the rate with the receptionist and agreed to stay for three days. I couldn't carry my stuff anymore, and I still did not know what I was doing with my life. I was excited by the prospect of a bed and took a nap straight away. With renewed energy, I ventured out to explore Torremolinos. It turns out that it isn't the nicest of places. It took me only five minutes to realise why people had been so surprised that I had been excited about English, there were English tourists everywhere. Package holiday people. And Swedes, so many Swedes! When I finally found the

---

[41] Mallorca, for the Spaniards.

beach, after a plethora of wrong turns through private property and resorts, I found it packed and decorated with touts and hotel's beach chairs. I had stumbled into a nightmare, and I had willingly signed up for three days of it.

Luckily, there was beer and baguettes and chorizo and olives. I tried to let the pleasure on my palate drown out life's other worries and concerns. But something was nagging at the back of my mind that I needed to deal with. I was finally back in Europe, I needed to talk to Karl. Five minutes was all that we got before the internet broke and he had to return to his students seeing as he'd just launched his sailing school. The sun set, I went to sleep.

I feasted on free breakfast. My roommate asked me three times if I was leaving the same day and suddenly an idea struck. I ventured to reception to cancel my stay. Only they don't do refunds. Looking bankruptcy in the eye, I opted to stay and went straight to the supermarket to buy more beer. And that's when I met Matty, the South African sailing and dive instructor. I followed him to a BBQ in the park that was right next to my failure of a hitchhiking spot. Seeing as he had been volunteering at the hostel for a while, the BBQ was filled with interesting people. It made the afternoon just about bearable. I tried to call Karl again in the evening and failed. The brokenness and lostness and emptiness of Torremolinos descended on me again and I went straight to bed.

I managed to Skype Mom and Ouma in the morning, but it was still too early to call Karl. I'd found a cheap flight to Sweden, but I didn't know if he wanted me there. I went for a walk and decided to check out the nearby harbours just in case there was a boat heading somewhere interesting. Boats were always the answer to all of life's problems. (Sometimes though, they were the problem too).

My glasses case broke. My hat broke. But I found a host of friendly people around who tried to help me solve all of my life dilemmas. I failed to find a boat. I failed to find new sunglasses or a case. I failed to find a hat. And I failed to find Wi-Fi so, even though it was my self-acclaimed "alcohol-free day," I bought beer. I didn't plan to drink them both, but when I got back to the hostel, the aloof English guy decided to start talking. His "almost girlfriend" was coming to visit and he was in good spirits. My beers went down so quickly as we exchanged love stories that I continued with the drinking. When he ventured off to give his slightly dubious high-paying massage, I went to find Wi-Fi to call Karl. Forget Majorca, I was going to Sweden!

❦

Leaving day! I was up way too early and super excited to be getting out of the town. I was not excited about the hitch, but I was leaving at last! Hungover, I stumbled past an old age home where I stopped to write a sign. And then to a foreign exchange where most of my foreign currencies were too foreign, so it took 46 minutes to up my wallet by seven euros and 56 cents. Finally, I reached a wall covered with beautiful flowers and I decided that it was going to be a magical day. It took over an hour to get my first ride and it didn't go anywhere close to where I wanted to head, but I needed to get away from Torremolinos.

My bag was heavy. And my heart may have added some extra weight, too. The sun upped its temperature, and life became hard. I plastered on my smile so that hopefully someone would see it and think, "Ah, look she's so happy, how can we not pick her up?" I changed my sign and tried again. There I was at a cactus-y intersection, stuck. I walked down the road trying to hold back my tears. It was too hot. I was exhausted. Nobody stopped. And then a bus did. But it left before I made it to the door. I almost cried again but held back the tears by stuffing my mouth with cookies I still carried from Morocco.

Finally, a car stopped and gave me a ride to the mall in Marbella. They were so friendly and funny that small flickers of hope returned to my being. An hour later I jumped in with a Dutch lady and then another. A Moroccan port official dropped me in Tarifa. Everyone had told me that it was a nice place, so I figured I might as well check it out. Seeing as I still had no idea where I was going, the best thing I could do was enjoy the journey while I searched for someplace to call home.

Tarifa was packed with Kite Surfers. While I searched for accommodation, I quickly learned that in Spain, not all "hostels" are Hostels. I wished I had a tent. After my friendly driver gave me a tour of the city, I took to foot to seek out affordable accommodation and finally booked myself in with the kite surfers. I was worried about all the youngsters but, while I was still checking in, I met Joost. The Brunei-born Dutchie had travelled the whole world thanks to his father's business. He invited me for dinner and for a moment I forgot about Karl and started imagining a future with Joost. But it was short-lived, we simultaneously lost interest in each other and started talking to other people. The whole hostel went out together and, seeing as German Theresa's only Spanish was, "Free shots for all!" we all got free shots everywhere we went.

Something had changed in me. There was a light that kept attracting people. It's amazing how a good place and open-hearted people can switch you back into life. I danced until three a.m. and met a plethora of beautiful people. I entertained the thought of living in Tarifa. Only I needed more than simple kite surfing and the prospect of bar hookups to keep me still. The hostel was a ghost town at breakfast, but I took my early start to set out and explore the city by daylight.

Pros
The old town is immaculate
There are cheap Chinese stores
Lidl
Happy people

Cons
It is far windier than Cape Town
The harbour has no sailing boats

Somewhere deep inside I knew it was not my place. It was nice, but there was still something lacking.

I spent the remainder of the day with Dutch Irini. I needed to meet her. I needed girl talk. I needed to talk boy. I needed to share my fears with her and hear hers. Her biggest fear is drowning. I then realised that my biggest fear was commitment. And specifically saying "I love you." I had still never uttered the words. I had tried to say it back to Karl because I did love him, but I wanted to mean it with every fibre of my being. When I tried to call him only a couple of days earlier to say those exact words, he hadn't answered the phone. Life has a funny way of working things out. Maybe I was meant to save it for someone else.

I couldn't afford another day at the Kite Surfing Hostel so it was a good thing Jeandré had messaged to suggest CouchSurfing. What better way to get to know a place than through the people who live there? I had been a member of CouchSurfing for over a decade, but I had still never used it. I tended to find places to stay organically through the people I met on the road. I had tried a few times before, but the people I had contacted, always wanted more notice than I ever had or they had been off travelling themselves. I contacted only one person in a nearby city who seemed to have a soul. Cali sent an immediate: "Yes! As long as you can be here before 17:00," so I packed my bags, hugged all my new friends goodbye, had a two-hour chat with the hostel owner about hostel success, and set off for Cadiz.

A French kite surfing champion gave me my first ride. And then, after an hour of side-of-the-road rejection, one of the Norwegians I had met on my bar crawl walked past and we went for coffee. He taught me that entrepreneurs are tunnel-visioned. He said that instead of doing a 20% life, 80% work balance, you really have to go in 50-50. The same went with marriage.

"Can I give you my criticism?" he asked.

I grimaced, but seeing as I was entering a new chapter of life and wanting to be the best person I could be, I accepted.

"You're an excellent mix of masculine and feminine energy," he said, "don't change that. Don't be like those other girls who sit and wait. Stay the way you are, go out and do."

He made sure I knew that he was happily married, and not coming onto me. He made me promise to remember to let someone into my life at some point. I bought the second round of coffee before he joined his friends on the beach. An hour and a half later they all laughed as I was still sitting there, patiently waiting. With a full round of hugs and a big smile on my face, they disappeared. Suddenly, it was like I had done what I needed to do in the Tarifa area, and a car arrived to whisk me onwards. A Spanish tattoo artist, former pirate, and fully awesome man in the driver's seat.

It took only ten carloads of rejection before some students picked me up and drove me to the University of Cadiz. It was 16:36 and I still had seven kilometres to go. I'm glad I missed the bus because the next lady who passed was going exactly where I needed to go and I arrived in town just after five. I found Wi-Fi and called. Seeing as Cali had just left home, he doubled back and came to find me. He let me in and showed me his apartment before he sped off to Seville. Only his car broke down so he didn't get very far.

It was a hungover start to the day, so I went for a run and then sprawled out on the balcony with my diary to spleen. I'm glad it was a foggy morning because it made me feel like I wasn't missing out on anything. I managed to catch up my travel diary so that my head and body could finally be in the same place at the same time.

As much as I should be in Palma to get a boat job, or in Sweden for midsummer to clarify the Karl thing once and for all, or in Portugal because that's where my heart is telling me to go, today I have a feeling that I am exactly where I need to be, and I am going to make the most of it.

The town sucked me in and I got lost in its awesomeness. I had a pang of plaguing guilt that I should touch base with my CouchSurfing host, but Wi-Fi was nowhere to be found. Also, Cadiz was awesome and I needed to see all of it. I seemed to be exuding some strange pheromones as old men kept coming to touch my face or knee. And I kept wishing I would attract a youngster instead. Maybe that's why the young Frenchman came and joined me at the beach.

I had wandered much further than I had thought and it took me forever to get home. And even longer because I kept on meeting fantastic people. Cali and I reached the front door at the same time. He apologised for being away for so long. I burst out laughing because we shared the same guilt but perfect timing.

Cali was right, I needed to lighten my load. I was carrying far too much in my pack and even more on my mind. I needed to let go! It was an emotional morning of de-cobwebbing my life with Cali. We had a lot in common, including dreams and burdens. He carried my pack as he walked me four blocks down to the fuel station. After a big hug, I had a two-hour wait to process my thoughts. I completely forgot why I had been standing there and was surprised when a truckie waved me over. We had great conversations despite not sharing a common language. We stopped three times to pick up goods for delivery and then he offered me a beer. The olive plantations began. My driver had an amazing ability to chug a beer in four sips and then throw the can out of the window. He did the same with a bag of clothes, scrutinising one item at a time and throwing them out. I was quickly being less awed by him. My over-active mind began to wonder if the clothes had belonged to his previous hitchhiker. At the first opportunity, I talked myself out of the truck and he wished me a good life. I was grateful that he had let me keep mine.

An Argentinian dropped me off at a fuel station near Seville where the temperature gauge rang out at 49 degrees (120 Fahrenheit). I escaped to Lidl for liquids before I continued my quest. I was back in survival mode, if nobody stopped, I would melt. I waved one seedy man off and took a big swig of water.

"¡Chica vamos!"

A BMW full of smiles and blaring music was welcoming me in. We didn't even try to talk, we just danced. They tried to teach me flamenco. I did as well as I could before they dropped me off at the traffic circle in Huelva. Five cars later I had a new friend, only I am not so sure he was a good kind of friend. I also suspect that the job he offered me would not make my mom proud.

A family came next, they were only going to the supermarket, but that was where I got my ride to the border. It was all in Spanish, but the radio was broadcasting the Soccer World Cup game between Sweden and Germany. Neither of us cared for soccer, but we were both too tired to talk. I simply sat and smiled as we crossed a mammoth bridge to my day's destination. I had made it to Portugal, which also happened to be the last stop on my heritage tour.

27

Home.

Unlike Spain, the second car to drive down the road in Portugal stopped and picked me up. The chef only spoke Portuguese and French, so that is how we tried to communicate. I was a little bit in love with the 44-year-old, even though we only spent ten minutes together. But then again, when you are in love with life, you tend to fall in love with everything else as well. 2018 seemed to be the year of the French.

I was dropped off in a small town. And I was still making a sign for Tavira (because Cali had recommended it and Cali was the sort of person whose recommendations should be listened to) when a family picked me up. They were headed for the mall so I took the opportunity to try and find a tent. One store and €14.99 later, I was ready for everything. I used the free Wi-Fi to try and find a host for the night so that I could get a proper introduction to Portugal, but there didn't seem to be a lot of CouchSurfing going on. I tried my luck anyway and shot off a few messages before I wandered off to find a beer, I'd just crossed another border and I needed to celebrate it.

Sufficiently hydrated, I tried to find a spot to pitch my tent, but the taverna owner found me and talked me out of it. He was nice enough to drive me to the hostel in town and became my guide to the city. He explained how it was a special day of celebration, something resembling Tavira's birthday. Dropped off at the hostel, the receptionist was more surprised than I was that there was an empty bed. And, after meeting Teddy, she gave me a hefty discount so that I could actually afford it. As if I wasn't already overjoyed to be in Portugal, the world exploded into fireworks as I finished the check-in! It was midnight and I was exhausted, but seeing as it was my first night in Portugal, I dragged myself out to explore and enjoy it.

Breakfast was a feast of good people, good food and too much coffee. After savouring it all, I opened up my laptop to try and make life plans. But the sun was shining and the world was calling my name, so I quickly gave up and went exploring. I lost myself in the rice paddies as I chatted to God. I felt like I was the murky water, I felt like I needed to sit still and settle. I sat in the shade of a tree to spleen. An old man approached and started chatting. He asked if I was married and then touched my face. Then he touched my leg. As he moved in for the boob, I whacked his hand and told him to get lost. I left too. Did I want to stay in Tavira or go? I asked a friendly local and he told me I should stay. So did my decision-making spinning top. I checked myself in for another night and had a nap, I needed the nap.

I had an afternoon beer in a park and another man approached similarly to the first creep. I yelled at him and after he had left me, the morning's old man found me again. I left. Did I look like a prostitute? My receptionist laughed in disbelief when I asked her. She reassured me. But when I exited the hostel, another old man pulled his car up next to me and tried to get me to climb in. Maybe when you are in love with life, everyone around you falls in love with you too?

I enjoyed the city, but something inside me told me that it wasn't the right place for me. But where should I go? My good friend Mary-Anne had good things to say about Lisbon. Seeing as I could not speak Portuguese and I needed a job, Lisbon was probably my only real option. I drifted off to sleep with peace and wondering, I was looking brokeness in the eye, and the next day would be a big one!

After an over-indulgent breakfast and still no CouchSurfing replies I had to decide between going back to bed or hitting the road. I looked myself in the mirror and gave myself a pep talk. My roommates came in while I was doing it. Instead of laughing, we got into a real conversation in no particular language. By the time I was actually leaving they seemed saddened to let me go. Juan thanked me for my inspiration and promised that he would return to Porto and quit his job because he knew he needed to enjoy life again. And the receptionist didn't let me off so easily either. She had a long list of questions about travel and life. We shared a common curiosity about the planet. I left laden with hugs and good vibes.

The first car drove me a little way out of town and assured me that I was on the right path. But there I waited an hour. Cars, trucks, four ambulances, two police bikes, more trucks, more cars. A Spaniard stopped, but I waved him on. And the next car that stopped, I waved on, too. Was my intuition working? Or was I being paranoid? The previous night another hostel dweller had told me how a friend of a friend had just been murdered hitchhiking. I waited. A van passed, went around the traffic circle twice and then stopped.

Andrei. The Romanian had moved to Spain at 16 and had already held 21 jobs in his 27 years of existence. He now made a living by lugging other Romanians across borders. He agreed to drive me the 56 kilometres to where he was set to pick up his next load. He didn't have all the paperwork and he got a couple of speeding fines every week, but he was still radiating life and was loving what he did. He told me to go back to Spain instead. Like so many I had already met, he tried to sell me Spain purely because the money was better there. I tried to assure him that there was more to life and money was not everything, but he wouldn't hear it and simply laughed it off.

He dropped me on the road to a town called Lagos. I turned around, had a wee at a café and then continued walking back to the road to Lisbon. It was hot! I stopped in the shade of a tree to recover. Wallace of the aeroplanes found me there and drove me five kilometres up the road and wished me good luck. Then it was German Claus who drove me another 800 meters and fed me figs from his garden. The taste alone made me know I was in my promised land. An English couple drove me another seven kilometres and told me to A) Give myself a bit of a break and B) Check out everything and anything in the Algarve before I moved on. I took their advice and had a beer break at a café while I tried to cool my body down and clear my head.

Only rejections came in from CouchSurfing requests for Lisbon. I sighed. At least there was no pressure to get there in any hurry. Looking out of the window of the Snack Bar, curiosity struck. I wondered what kind of people lived in the hot middle of nowhere where I currently sat. The first profile I clicked on was so ridiculously cool, interesting and inspiring that I sent an immediate request. I needed to meet this guy. I didn't hold my breath though, I was learning through experience that most people never even checked their requests.

Forty-seven minutes later, I met Mark at the church. The world championship bike racer was even cooler in real life than his profile had made him out to be. I lost myself in conversation because there were too many things I wanted to know at the same time. Why Portugal? How was he going to run his farm and cyclist/ hiker retreat? How was he going to market it? What other jobs was he doing on the side? How long had he been in a wheelchair? What did he want to eat for dinner? That was all on the way to his home, his slice of paradise.

I was blown away by the terrace alone. The vibe, the view, the potential. It was all amazing in the afternoon sun. His house was spectacular, even the upstairs, where he had never been. And then the fruit trees and the garden. He tended to it all himself, from the wheelchair. After a feast of food, we went for what he called "a walk". I fell in love with the Algarve. Mark invited me to stay an extra day to catch my head up with my body. And, after cleaning and sorting all my belongings, I started cleaning my soul. I didn't realise how broken it was. I was a new human by the time Mark got home from work. He could see the differences in me after only knowing me a day. Sometimes we simply have to stop and do nothing so that we can actually progress. The logic of this is sound, even if it does not sound like it.

The following morning Mark dropped me off at a fuel station on his way to work. I crossed the road to start hitching with my Lisbon sign. I got a ride from a man on his way to work in the mountains, he detoured a little to drop me off on the highway. That's where Maria found me and picked me up. She didn't care where I wanted to go, she was taking me to Lagos. I tried to explain that I wanted Lisbon. But she was very firm in her answer, "No, not Lisbon. You will come to Lagos."

There was no arguing with her. We drove into a dusty car park and walked down the road to the shop she was managing. She made me take a photo of the "staff wanted" sign. She told me to come back without all my stuff and with shoes for an interview. She smiled and added that it was better to leave Teddy behind too. I hugged her goodbye unsure if she was crazy or awesome.

I continued down the road towards the water. With every step, I felt more and more at home. Could she be right? Could Lagos really be where I needed to be? I walked towards the boats, left my bags and bear at the marina office and went exploring.

I felt like a new woman, lightly loaded, springing down the streets. I smiled excessively because it was a good day and Lagos held great vibes. None of the plethora of sales vendors tried to sell me a tour, not one. They could sense my gypsy. I chatted to a few of the boating and sailing companies but they all required Portuguese licenses to work on boats. It didn't deter my spirit and by the end of the Marina, I had mild success. The owner agreed to meet me at one p.m. for an interview. As I walked back toward town, I bumped straight into the World ARC crowd. Terry was a walking smile and while we shared the walk we laughed and joked.

"Are you for real?" he asked when I inquired about space on his boat. He handed me his card and said we could talk. He invited me to their arrival celebration drinks happening later that night.

I finally bought a SIM card, to rejoin society, and once more became the proud owner of a telephone number. But my joy was short-lived as I jammed it in the wrong card slot. I tried and tried to get it out, as did the friendly salesman, but there was no luck. He redirected me to a repair shop. I walked across town and handed a youngster my phone. Four minutes later it was fully functional and it cost me nothing.

"Just have a nice day," said the young repairman.

My smile grew. I loved Lagos. That was the defining moment when I knew I had to give Lagos a try.

I stopped at a hostel to see about working for accommodation. They had no place for me but sent me to someone who might. Could I clean? Probably. Only they couldn't give me accommodation. I said I'd return later for more information and ran back across town to the far side of the marina for my first interview. I was offered the job, but it was part-time. I thanked the man and set off to sort out my life. Where was I going?

I pin-balled across town as people sent me between the rigmarole of hostels that decorated the city. There were plenty of job offers as a cleaner, but no accommodation. As much as on the surface it all looked like "no", I had already made up my mind with a definite "yes" to stay and discover the town[42].

I smiled my way past all the vendors for the umpteenth time and entered the marina office to collect my stuff. I was about to check myself into the cheapest hostel I had found when some fellow-gypsies called me over. I shared their litre beer as we chatted. They convinced me that the hostel was wrong for me and that the campsite would be much better. It was not. But it did add many extra steps to my existence. I followed them, pitched my tent, and ran back across town again to meet the posh yachties for their celebratory drinks.

Terry was an awesome character, but the rest of the group made me weary and reminded me why I had avoided these kinds of gatherings in the past. I was broke, and I was about to reside in a tent, but I had found the first place I wanted to call home. Suddenly I didn't want to sail away anymore. I returned to my tent and cooked up the lentils I still carried from *Turia*, trying to take in what was happening in life and thinking that it was probably best to sleep on it.

The campsite was noisy, but I woke up refreshed and early seeing as there was no way to sleep in. I chatted with some of the other inmates and decided that I didn't want to share their fate, so I ventured out to find a job

---

[42] By Portuguese standards, it is recognised as a city as it has a sizable population, good infrastructure (schools, medical care, cultural and sports facilities) and historical importance.

and better accommodation. Finally, a vendor stopped me. But he didn't want to sell me anything, he simply wanted to introduce himself so that he could ask why I was smiling so much.

"Adeena," I said, smiling even more.

"Henk."

I liked Henk. He was one of those greater than life, work hard, play harder kind of people. A few minutes later another Dutchman stopped me and invited me to see his boat. I followed him and enjoyed some morning champagne that came with an interesting accommodation proposal. I could share the boat in exchange for a couple of cuddles and some fancy dinners. I would even have my own room, but the 80-something-year-old needed company and wanted kisses. That's how I realised that I definitely wasn't desperate. I thanked him for the offer and the drink and ran. Maybe my solution wasn't boats after all?

My phone started ringing while I ran. Could I come by a hostel for an interview? I said I would be right there, but I didn't know yet how many distractions Lagos held and how long it would take me to get across the town. Fortunately, Lagos is the final frontier of Europe and close enough to run on African time. I got the job and was set to start first thing in the morning. Then I panicked, I didn't want to be a cleaner! I printed out a few copies of my résumé and ran around town in desperation to find something more fun. Most of the bars and restaurants weren't open yet because it was still early, so I stuck my head into the surf shop on the corner just to ask them if they knew of anyone who was looking for staff.

That one chance encounter was exactly where I needed to be! I found Wi-Fi and power and put my affairs in order before continuing to run around the town like a crazy person. A person who knew that it was their last day of freedom and was unsure if they were ready for the commitments coming their way.

I had told Terry I would meet him for a beer, so I ran back to the marina. I was late and found more people wanting crew instead. I was being tested, and given the opportunity to fall back into old ways. Only I already knew that I didn't want to sail straight back to the Caribbean. I wanted land. I wanted community. I wanted Lagos. Terry understood the draw: the need for water and adventure and the thirst for land. He was privileged enough to enjoy both. I hugged him and started back to my tent, only to hear my name.

"Adeena."

I was sure I was imagining it, but I heard it again. There sat Henk and his friends and they waved me over to join them. A few beers later we stumbled in our different directions and my smile continued to grow.

I stopped at the supermarket and spent my last euro on two beers and returned to sneak into the campsite because I could no longer afford to pay for the night. I handed one beer to my new neighbour and cheered him as I cooked up my couscous and lentils and wondered what the flip I was doing with my life. I was officially broke.

I was nervous about my first day as a cleaner. South Africans pay other people to clean their houses. South Africans are the worst cleaners. But the hostel was so dirty that I needn't have worried. They could not have cared less about the state of the hostel and merely wanted the essentials done. No! I didn't have to change sheets unless they were blood-stained or shitty.

"Faster. The bins! Why are you spending so much time in the corners?"

At some point, I found the Wi-Fi password and connected. *Could I come in for a trial shift at Jah Shaka Surf Shop at 8:30 tomorrow?* I sent an immediate "Yes," but pushed the time a bit later because another day of cleaning loomed ahead. I got yelled at for being on my phone, so I cleaned like my life depended on it and thanked God that this job would be short-lived. My accomplice in crime hated the job, too. But he tried to sell me on the benefits. And to be paid daily definitely was a benefit when you only have a few copper cents to your name and less than a euro in your bank account.

I survived my first day of cleaning and, feeling relatively rich, I headed to the marina to buy Henk a thank-you drink. Only the spirits at the marina were low and nobody I knew was anywhere to be found, so I turned the other way and headed toward the campsite. (I can't call it home because it definitely was not.) I took a different route, and that's when I found the beach. Would you believe that I had already decided on Lagos before I had even seen the magical alleyways and tunnels and rock formations that make the place utterly gorgeous? Who cares if I was a cleaner, I had found paradise! And I had it all to myself as the full moon rose and the last colour dissolved from the sky.

I sat down on a tiny secluded beach in awe. I feasted on Piri-piri chicken and sipped on my litre beer. I cheered God and thanked Him for life. For Lagos. For Home. I had finally found *my home*.

UNEMPLOYMENT LOOKS BETTER WITH A TAN

000

Lagos

It took me a couple of years and even more accidental adventures until I finally settled in Lagos. I nearly circled the world again in my stubbornness. I wanted to see all of it, just to make sure that I had found the perfect place to live.

There is no such thing as perfect. There are no perfect places. There are no perfect people. I did not need to be perfect. And, as much as I believe that all things are possible, conditions will never be perfect.

It's a beautiful thing watching all the seasons pass and how the landscape changes with it. I used to follow summer as if it was the only season that mattered. But seeds are never sown in summer. And winter is when we find rest and appreciation for warm fires. Time for creativity. Autumn is for slowing down and changing leaves (and wardrobes[43]). And Spring for rebirth. Settling in Lagos was like a rebirth.

---

[43] Especially when you stop living out of a backpack!

> ### *A Time for Everything*
>
> *There is a time for everything,*
> *and a season for every activity under the heavens:*
>
> *² a time to be born and a time to die,*
> *a time to plant and a time to uproot,*
> *³ a time to kill and a time to heal,*
> *a time to tear down and a time to build,*
> *⁴ a time to weep and a time to laugh,*
> *a time to mourn and a time to dance,*
> *⁵ a time to scatter stones and a time to gather them,*
> *a time to embrace and a time to refrain from embracing,*
> *⁶ a time to search and a time to give up,*
> *a time to keep and a time to throw away,*
> *⁷ a time to tear and a time to mend,*
> *a time to be silent and a time to speak,*
> *⁸ a time to love and a time to hate,*
> *a time for war and a time for peace.*
>
> *- Ecclesiastes 3:1-11*

Instead of scribbling away in my travel diary about insecurities and all the things I really wanted, I found a community to stand with me. People who helped me tackle things face-on. A tribe who accepted and loved me, no matter how weird I was or how many mistakes I made. (Learning that people can love you despite all your flaws has been a tough lesson.) People who push me towards my goals and help me believe that even my wildest dreams can be reality.

After so many years spent living in survival mode, it has been prodigious to simply be "safe." Instead of worrying about battling the elements and scrounging for food, I have lived in abundance and peace. Apart from the hangovers, Lagos is one of the safest places on earth, in every respect. And with it being the end of the railway line in Europe, it is one of the most eclectic places, too.

Still, sitting "still" has been one of the most challenging adventures yet. I have to keep fighting my itchy feet so they can grow some roots. "Real life" can be just as exciting as travel, and I have been trying to keep it that way.

I still keep diaries and I still have adventures abroad, but every time I come back here, I know that I am home. Yes, home can be everywhere, but to have a safe base and community that you can keep coming back to is different.

Maybe the best way to deal with heartache isn't to run from it. Maybe it is to sit still and let difficult emotions and unresolved issues catch up with you so you can combat them forever. And learn from them. And at the same time build community to help you grow. Maybe the best way to deal with heartache is to let your heart beat again.

ADEENA GERDING

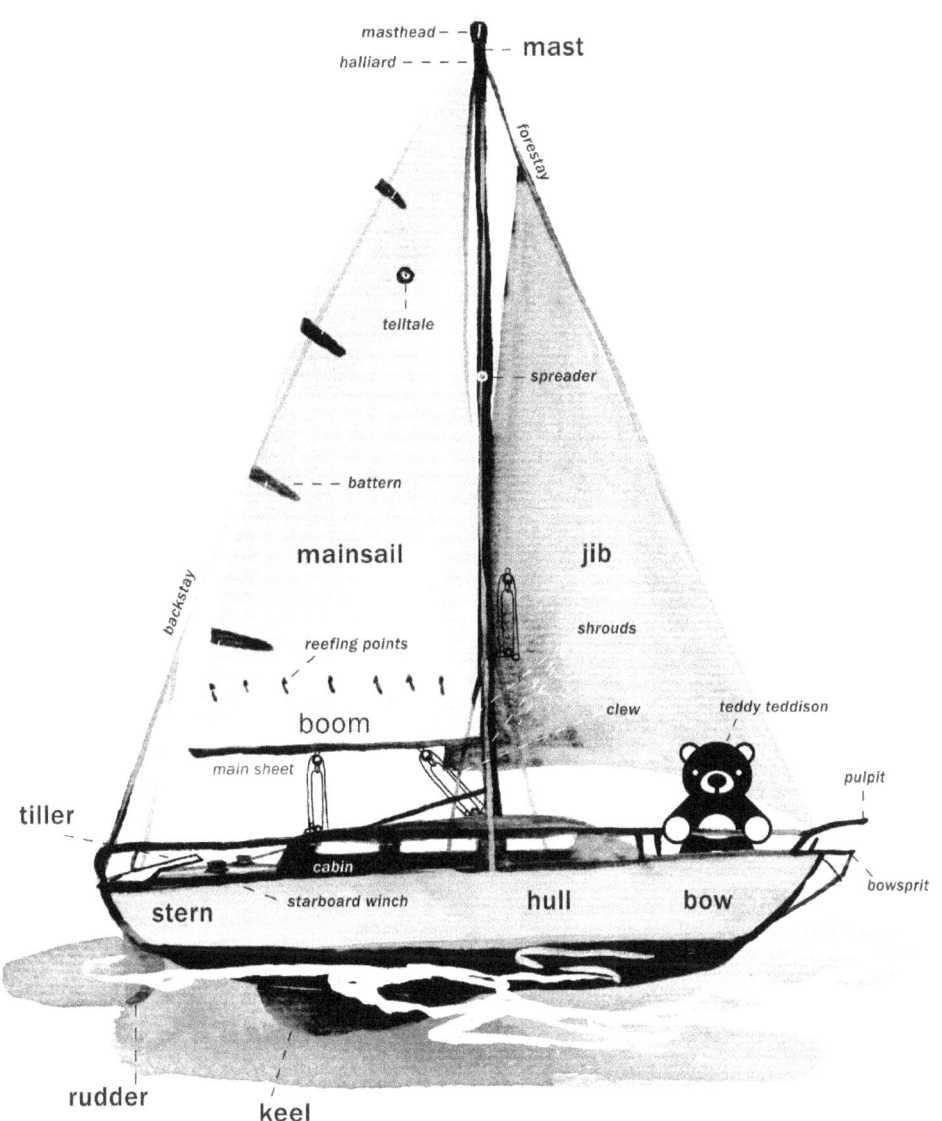

Intention

(Just in case I forget why I am going home)

I am going home to water my roots.
To delve in and immerse myself in the colour and beats and diversity of South Africa.
To become part of the community
To reconnect with old friends and family.
And make new ones.
To surround myself with people who will challenge, explore and laugh with me.
While pushing me forward towards undiluted awesomeness.

I intend to find fun and exciting ways to avoid being a drain on society or broke or homeless or starving to death.

To find gainful employment that resonates with my soul.
And still allows funds and freedom for adventure.

I want to write [travel books] that will evoke salivation for the unknown and inspire epic. Books that will challenge others while still being a good read.

I want to acquire my own boat and shape her to perfection. To live on her, give her personality, and give her wings.
I want to gift people a lustre for the ocean. Teach them how to sail and explore and fully live.

I want a base where I am free to invite people for as long as they like.
I want to have fun and purpose and feel flipping good.
Physically, mentally, and spiritually.

I intend to live a life worthy of my calling.
Home should be even more epic than my travels!

Acknowledgements

M*y journey has been paved with so many exceptional people* and experiences that there is no way that I could begin to mention them all on these pages without unnecessary deforestation!

To all those who played an integral part in helping me shape and tell this story, THANK YOU!

Annie, not only did you sit beside me when I struck challenging memories, but by making our respective book launches a competition, I didn't dare to lose to find out what kind of book tour you had schemed up for me. (I hope you like the cold :)

Lynn, you have been a Godsend! Thank you for not only stealing me from my former vessel, brightening up my life, and sharing my faith,

UNEMPLOYMENT LOOKS BETTER WITH A TAN

but for battling my grammar and malapropisms, too. If I had not met you and Todd when I did, I fear I may not have survived to tell this tale!

Mary-Anne, this book would have been incomplete without your cover and images and the backing support for years of neurotic phone calls! (I promise I'll be on the phone again soon with more life drama.)

Derek Murphy, thank you for providing the template for this book and for your invaluable writing coaching.

To Lurdes, Alexis, and Pie, thank you for graciously hosting and organising my book launch. Your efforts made the event truly special.

To those who bravely allowed me to include their very real and sometimes painful stories, thank you. In a world where some topics are often swept under the rug, your willingness to open up and share is truly commendable. Together, we're breaking down barriers and letting others know they're not alone in their struggles.

To the many people I have crewed with over the years, thank you for sharing adventures and enduring my chilli-loaded dishes! Kirk and James, I'll forever be grateful for your invitation aboard *Fiddler*, even if it did come with a slightly tilted perspective on the ocean. Thank you to all past and future crew members for accepting my raging emotions and celebrating my arbitrary milestone celebrations :).

Karl, I still cannot believe how much we endured! Thank you for remaining true and inspirational through all the chapters of your own life, those that overlapped with mine, as well as those that did not.

To all those I have pedalled alongside, you have experienced the true brunt of my hangryness[44], yet we have somehow remained friends! Thank you

---

[44] Hungry-anger-fullness.

for sharing miles of road and impromptu campsites with me!

To all the others I have travelled, hitchhiked, beer-ed, dined, danced, sang, sank, stowed away, run, chilled, beached, swum, and made out with; thank you for brightening up my journey and my life!

To the many, many drivers who have stopped to pick me up along the road, I'm so glad I had those moments where our lives could intersect (also, thank you for not killing me)!

To all those who employed me and worked with me, thank you for adding such rich experiences to my "settled" life (and for lining my pockets.) Thank you to all those I worked and lived alongside at The Great Aussie Bush Camp.

Chris, Mel, Griff, Lucas, Eli, Joao, Tony and all the rest of the crew at Jah Shaka Surf Shop; thank you for all the good times! And for all those I worked random jobs with in-between; thank you!

To the inhabitants of Lagos, thank you for creating a place where my Gypsy soul feels like it belongs! From the bartenders to the beggars to the coffee barristers; and all those who have simply sat and sipped tasty beverages over a conversation. To live in an ever-transforming non-clicky town full of smiles and engaging conversation is a blessing.

Thank you to all my teachers: dance, drumming, boxing... your patience deserves a medal! Dolphins, I am going to thank you too with the hope that you will visit our shores more frequently.

To all the wonderful souls who have opened their homes to me, whether for a single night or several months, thank you! A special shoutout to those like Paula and the van der Wals, who not only provided the shelter and electricity needed for me to pen this tale but also shared their warmth and hospitality. To all the fantastic individuals I've had the pleasure of living

UNEMPLOYMENT LOOKS BETTER WITH A TAN

with under these roofs, your kindness has left an indelible mark on my journey. And to The Studio Coffee, your piripiri cappuccino remains unparalleled—thank you for the caffeinated bliss!

Thank you to all of you who have prayed me through horrific circumstances and near-death experiences! I am glad that my time has not yet come and I hope to keep making the most of all the days I have left.

To my family and teachers (both formal and informal). Thank you for preparing me to take on the world!

Thank you to all the friends who have believed in and supported me. And to those who have not, thank you for allowing me to prove you wrong :)

Jeandré and Brendon (and Chloe and AJ) thank you for being amazing siblings. And thank you for so many awesome adventures, may life throw us many more!

Ouma, thank you for being the most inspirational grandmother and for all the time you have spent on your knees!

Mom. I'm sorry that this is how you had to find out the finer details of my former epics. Thank you for trying to talk me out of them. And thank you for praying me through them when I have failed to take your advice.

God, there is no way I could have endured any of this without you.

I love you all! And no matter what the future holds, remember that you're exactly where you're meant to be. You'll always have enough, and most importantly, remember: everything looks better with a tan, even unemployment!

About the Author

BORN AND RAISED, like most people, Adeena's journey began amidst the bustling streets of Johannesburg. In addition to mastering the art of breathing and walking (albeit occasionally in circles), she also conquered other essential life phenomena like swimming and math—which proved particularly useful for deciphering cryptic street signs and calculating the odds of missing her train by exactly two minutes. And while Johannesburg was way too far away from the ocean for her liking, it was the perfect springboard for her to dabble in a little bit of everything

Curious about the outside world, Adeena hesitantly agreed to join some friends on an adventure through Africa in 2007. What was initially intended as a three-month trip quickly transformed into an addiction—to both adrenaline and the word 'yes'. Consequently, Adeena found herself accidentally cycling across some continents, hitchhiking across others, and allowing the whims of the wind to carry her around the world more than once. (Though, admittedly, the wind also had a knack for tossing her around quite a bit).

While unemployment has been a recurring theme in her life (seriously, who needs a time limit for adventure?), Adeena has tackled a plethora of random jobs in various countries, crafting a resume that's more eclectic than a thrift store bargain bin.

Adeena's most notable accomplishments to date include not only surviving (a feat that deserves its own medal) but also mastering the fine art of making mistakes—often spectacularly. Currently attempting to plant some roots in Portugal (figuratively, of course), she's also delving into the world of Adventure Therapy, amongst other things. And while she's still undecided about what she wants to be if she grows up, one thing's for sure: being an "adult" is definitely not on the list of options.

You can find out more about Adeena's [mis]adventures and life at
www.bearfootgypsy.com

Thanks for reading!
Please add a short review on Amazon or Goodreads and let me know what you thought!

www.ingramcontent.com/pod-product-compliance
Lightning Source LLC
Chambersburg PA
CBHW062046290426
44109CB00027B/2748